AF526642

The Mother of All Beings

Books in English by the Author (besides 12 books in Bengla)

Biography and Essays

- *Sri Aurobindo's Ideal of Freedom and Human Unity*
- *Sri Aurobindo: The Yogi of Divine Life*
- *The World of Sri Aurobindo's Creative Literature* (in Press)
- *Lord Ganesha*
- *Contemporary Indian English Poets: Thoughts and Discourses* (in Press)

Poems

- *The Witness Tree*
- *In Celebration of Nature*
- *The Paper Boat*
- *Short Verse Vast Universe*
- *Aju Mukhopadhyay's Poems on Sri Aurobindo and the Mother*
- *Insect's Nest and Other Poems*
- *Short Verse Delight*

Short Stories and Novel

- *White Bird and its Black Shadow*
- *The Moments of Life*
- *In Train*

Environmental

- *Pondicherry Environment*

Current Topics

- *India the Mother: Unity Diversity Integrity* (in Press)

The Mother of All Beings

Aju Mukhopadhyay

AUTHORSPRESS

Worldwide Circulation through Authorspress Global Network
First Published (enlarged) 2012
by
Authorspress

Editorial
Q-2A Hauz Khas Enclave
New Delhi-110 016

Marketing
E-35/103, Jawahar Park
Laxmi Nagar, Delhi-110 092

e-mails: authorspress@rediffmail.com; authorspress@hotmail.com
Website: www.authorspressbooks.com

Copyright © 2012 Author

The Mother of All Beings
ISBN 978-81-7273-667-5

Printed in India at Tarun Offset, Delhi.

Dedicated to
those who realized or want to realize
the Mother's True Being

Preface

Mother of all Beings was published in 2002. Considerable time has lapsed since then. The number of devotees and enthusiastic readers of the Mother have increased in me meantime. So it is in the nature of things to publish this again. But in the process of revision a thorough rearrangement of chapters have been made to make it more relevant and in response to the demand of time three more chapters: 'Mother's Homecoming', 'Mother's Work' and 'Mother Said' have been added to make it an enlarged new book *The Mother Of All Beings*. My aim is to reach those who wish to realise or have realised the Mother as a human being with divine consciousness; both human and divine.

I am grateful to all others in the Authorspress who worked for this book but specially to Sudarshan Kcherry, the Managing Director, who had voluntarily undertaken to publish the book before I could complete the job and has taken personal interest in its publication. I offer my heartfelt thanks to them.

Aju Mukhopadhyay

Contents

1

Our Mother

Mirra Alfassa had passed through different phases of her life and gained invaluable experiences without any preplanned programme. She lived from wonder to wonder. She was a trained occultist, a musician, an artist, a speaker, a writer and a great organiser. The creation of Sri Aurobindo Ashram was her greatest organisational work. She became known as the Mother by all. She embodied a divine personality in her human form. She was a golden bridge between the earth and heaven. She lived to go beyond life.

Said Pinto, her great grandfather, was an Egyptian prince. He succeeded his father Mehemet Ali as the Viceroy of Egypt. He only permitted the digging of the Suez Canal which was opened in 1869 after his death. His ancestors were from Spain. Pinto's daughter, Mira Ismalun's husband had some roots in the Ural-Ultike region of Hungary. Mira's daughter Mathilde married Maurice Alfassa, a Turk who was a banker by profession. Maurice was brought up in Austria. Maurice and Mathilde, disgusted with life in Egypt, with all its restrictions and prejudices, moved to Paris in 1877. It took another 12 years for them to get a French citizenship.

Mirra Alfassa, their daughter, was born on a Thursday, 21 February 1878, at 10.15 am at 41, Boulevard Haussmann, Paris. A little while after the birth of his third child the nurse came to Maurice to ask for a name for the newborn baby. He immediately wrote "Mirra Alfassa," on a big cloth. And the nurse scribbled it down in a short form- M.A. Thus the nickname of the child became M.A. The word 'ma', means mother in many languages. Mirra became Ma or Mother from her birth.

Mira Ismalum was a vivacious woman who disliked growing old. Mathilde, her daughter was straightforward, headstrong and progressive. Her husband was physically very strong with a tremendous brain for mathematics. He was fond of adventures and loved to relate to his children tales of adventure as he had read in books, making them his own. But they were down-to-earth and practical. They did not care for the existence of God. Mathilde absolutely repudiated the invisible.

Mirra's formal education including physical training continued side by side with her inner development. At the age of five she would sit for hours in a chair specially made for her, and feel the pressure of light and force above her head. Her *sadhana* began from birth: "I began my *sadhana* at birth, without knowing that I was doing it. I have continued it throughout my life. . . . But I began a deliberate, conscious *sadhana* at about the age of twenty-two or twenty-three, upon prepared ground."[1]

"When I was a child of about thirteen, for nearly a year every night as soon as I had gone to bed it seemed to me that I went out of my body and rose straight up above. Then I used to see myself clad in a magnificent golden robe, much longer than myself; and as I rose higher, the robe would stretch, spreading out in a circle around me to form a kind of immense roof over the city. Then I would see men, women, children, old men, the sick, the unfortunate coming out from every side; they would gather under the outspread robe, begging for help, telling of their miseries, their suffering, their hardships. In reply, the robe, supple and alive, would extend towards each one of them individually, and as soon as they had touched it, they were comforted or healed, and went back into their bodies happier and stronger than they had come out of them. Nothing seemed more beautiful to me, nothing could make me happier; and all the activities of the day seemed dull and colourless and without any real life, beside this activity of the night which was the true life for me."[2]

The people in her dreams throughout her life always approached her for help. Even as late as on 17 July 1963 when she was 85, she said in one of her conversations that showers of letters had been coming from known and unknown sources, from people who described their miseries, imploring her for her blessings. During the only time when she rested, between 2 and 4-30 a.m., she used to see people whom she had never seen before physically. She used to travel to places she had never known.

When she was about 12, she would go to the woods of Fontainbleu near her home, and sit at the feet of very old and giant trees, resting herself against their thick gnarled trunks, roots. Though she did not know what meditation was, she often used to be merged in communion with nature. Squirrels would sit on her shoulders and birds perch on her head, and after hours of such meditation she would open her eyes to find a gazelle intently looking at her. She became a great lover of nature.

Mirra, having completed her regular schooling at the age of 15, joined the Academie Julian as a student of Art. She began to draw at the age of eight, started oil painting at 10, and was doing portraits by the age of 12. She was a talented artist. She had her studio. Some of her paintings were exhibited and sold at the famous 'Salon de la Societe National de Beaux Arts' in Paris. She married a senior artist, Henri Morisset on 13 October 1897. They were divorced in 1908. This period of her life as an artist was one of intense vital and artistic growth. She had known many famous artists to whom she was like a sister. She gradually immersed herself into occult life from 1905. But she did not altogether give up art. She did some oil paintings in Japan during the period from 1916 to 1920 and made many remarkable drawings in Pondicherry. From time to time she formed groups of elites who were intrigued by the invisible, who thought of philosophy, ethics and the higher principles of life. The young people usually met at her house. Madam Alexandra David Neel, a great occultist of Tibetan experience, was a member of her group called 'L'déa'; 'Le Cosmic' was another such group. At Pondicherry she organised 'L'déa Nouvelle', during the early part of her stay here.

Mirra met Max Theon at Paris in 1905 and travelled to Algeria in 1906 and 1907. There she learnt occultism very systematically from Max and Madam Alma Theon and soon became an expert. Many extraordinary things happened there. Moving out of the body and taming the turbulent sea were a few things she accomplished. Once, while remaining in Algeria, she appeared to a circle of friends sitting in Paris, took up a pencil and wrote a few words on a piece of paper. Then she signed her name and even moved an object.

Monsieur Paul Richard, an intellectual, too was interested in occultism. He travelled to Algeria and started working together with Mirra. They were married in 1911. While her life with Henri Morisset had been intensely vital and physical, it became mental, intellectual and occult from 1908 onwards, up to the time she met Sri Aurobindo. Paul Richard visited Pondicherry for some political reason and met Sri Aurobindo in 1910. He was very impressed by the presence of the yogi. He called him the Light of Asia. After the visit, Mirra started communication with Sri Aurobindo. During sleep and meditation she used to see luminous beings in the subtle world, who guided her in the spiritual domain. When Madam Mirra Richard came to Pondicherry for the first time and met Sri Aurobindo on 29 March 1914, she immediately recognised him as the Guru she often met whom she called Krishna, without even knowing much about India. During their meeting, both of them plunged into deep meditation. Later Mirra explained that she had a perfect silence before Sri Aurobindo, which she had always longed for but had never experienced. And Sri Aurobindo too admitted that he had never seen such a perfect surrender as Mirra's, which was so essential for his Integral Yoga. In course of time, Sri Aurobindo realised the divine presence in Mirra and announced her as the Mother. "You are She", he said. She became his collaborator in his efforts to bring down the supramental light and force upon earth.

The great quarterly magazine *Arya*, and its French counterpart, *Revue de Ia Grande Synthese,* started from 15 August 1914 with the collaboration of Monsieur and Madam Richard. Major portions of Sri Aurobindo's social, philosophical, and yogic treatise were published in the pages of *Arya* which continued to be published up to 1920. The Richards remained in Pondicherry up to 21 February 1915, Mirra's birthday. But they had to leave for France the next day under political compulsions. After a short stay in Europe in 1916 they went to Japan and remained there till the early part of 1920. Her earnest desire to come back to Pondicherry and to work with Sri Aurobindo to fulfil her spiritual mission brought her back permanently to Pondicherry on 24 April 1920.

At first she stayed separately but a severe cyclone at one night damaged a portion of her house and brought her to the place where Sri Aurobindo was staying with a few of his disciples. This was the 24 of November 1920. On 22 January next year Mother took charge of Sri Aubobindo's household along with some disciples. On 24 November 1926, the Siddhi day, when Sri Aurobindo realised the overmental consciousness in himself, he declared that thenceforth Mother would look after the affairs as In-charge. It may be said to be the foundation day of the Sri Aurobindo Ashram though there was no formal declaration about it.

The Ashram school started functioning from 1943. In 1951 was founded the Sri Aurobindo International Centre of Education. The foundation of Aruoville, an international township, was laid on 28 February 1968 as per Mother and Sri Aurobindo's ideal. It belongs to no nation, no religion, no race but to humanity, based on a higher spiritual sense. The project was recognised by UNESCO; 124 countries and 23 Indian provinces and union territories sent their earth to begin a new life for a new humanity.

The Ashram and all other institutions which grew up under Mother's leadership and guidance became unique in human history. Activities which were accepted in the Ashram are education, sports, agriculture, industrial manufacture, art and literature under Mother's guidance. Spiritual activity was the life-blood of the Ashram but it was not the exclusive activity. The Ashram is not the house of sannyasins as Sri Aurobindo conceived it. "All life is yoga", he said. All things are to be done selflessly with an attitude of inner renunciation.

Mother was a teacher, teaching at the school, and guiding other teachers. She often managed to get the required funds by selling her own ornaments. She planned everything and executed them through her disciples. Her activities were not limited to the Ashram but were spread to distant areas of the globe. She managed everything with a subtle spiritual and intuitive sense and understanding. Benevolence and goodwill were her weapons. A few examples of her divine ministry are given below as culled by M.P. Pandit in his *Sidelights on the Mother*.

1. The Honesty Engineers and Contractors had started with Mother's clear instructions to strictly adhere to all the estimates given to and accepted by the party, even if there would be price escalation at a later stage. Once it was found out that the cost of construction was actually lower than the estimate submitted and accepted by the party. Mother gave instructions to return the balance amount.
2. An old car was disposed of at a reasonable price during the Second World War. Hearing about the criticism that the car could have fetched a higher price, she replied that she had known it but not wished to profit out of a war situation.
3. She went to visit a department of the Ashram. All things were kept tidied. As she was being guided to the office, she moved towards the shed and asked what was there. Heaps of dried coconut shells and other junk were found. On being questioned later she said that as soon as she had reached the compound, she had heard a call from the shed- "Look at us, look how they have kept us."
4. A huge tree in one of Ashram bungalows was to be cut down. When the *sadhak* approached her for permission, she asked him to let the tree alone. Its spirit had come to her the previous night, imploring her to prevent the felling. Many such trees had been saved from her Fontainbleu-wood days.

K.M. Munshi, once a student of Aurobindo Ghose and later a cabinet Minister and Governor of U.P., visited the Ashram for the second time after Sri Aurobindo's departure, in March 1952. The result was an article in *The Hindustan Times* on 15 August 1952.

Mother said to him, "We are determined—he and I—to complete what he lived for."

He wrote among other things, "Suppose this French-born lady were exactly the same in other ways, but dressed in the saffron coloured robes of a sannyasin . . . the Mother stood on her head in *shirshasan* and spun the charkha—and if the ashramites ground their own flour instead of having it ground through a machine, what would have been our judgement?

"India would have gone on her knees before her in ardent devotion."

Mother had much illness in her body. On most occasions she cured herself. But gradually the body was failing more and more. She withdrew herself from all outer activities. By 6 December 1958 she stopped attending to her Wednesday, Friday and Translation classes. She played lawn tennis, her most favourite game, last on 7 December of that year, at the age of 80. After that she seldom came out of her room, but supervised the affairs of the Ashram through her disciples. She took very little rest throughout the day and night. Beyond all such routine work she was also engaged in her spiritual work. Once she mentioned to her disciple what Sri Aurobindo had said to her before his withdrawal from the body, "Your body is indispensable for the work. Without your body the work cannot be done."[3]

She remained after Sri Aurobindo for another 23 years. She had been drawing the divine light and influence in each cell of her body, to transform them. The Supramental consciousness had settled in her body after Sri Aurobindo's departure. She was working with that. She achieved the transformation of matter to the extent possible until the last day of her earthly life on 17 November 1973. That was the most important work that she was doing.

Mother was more than a genius. She could be at the acme of many human activities, but she cared little to become so. It would be a simple matter for her to be a champion. When she was young she always acted or played with her superiors to learn things better. She had her consciousness always awake to the fact of her statement which she uttered to her disciple, almost in a whisper: "You know, we belong to eternity!"

"Do not ask questions about the details of the material existence of this body: they are in themselves of no interest and must not attract attention," she said on 22 June 1958. It is left to us to realise who the Mother really was.

Once in her advanced age when in conversation to her disciple Mother said, "The body by itself has more than a feeling, a kind of . . . it is a knowledge- more than a knowledge, it is a fact: there are many, many beings, forces, personalities who manifest themselves through it, even sometimes several at the same time. That is a very common experience; we know, for example, that Sri Aurobindo is there, he speaks and sees, he has his own way of seeing and expressing himself, that happens very often. And then often it is Durga or Mahakali or . . . very often. Often it is a being from very high up, very permanent- very permanent—who manifests himself, and then there occurs a kind of absolute in the being. Sometimes it is beings from a plane nearby who try to make themselves felt, express themselves, but that is under control."[4]

Mother not only looked after with all care human disciples and devotees and other beings like animals, even plants during her earthly ministry but also sheltered various invisible beings.

The time of Sri Aurobindo and Mother may be called the Golden Era of the Ashram. Even then it had to pass through different difficult phases from time to time; faithlessness, mistrust and chaos tried to raise their ugly heads. The greatness of the masters' spiritual influence carried it through many vicissitudes. Much water has flown since. The Ashram has not remained the same. The enormous outgrowth of other interests has created serious imbalances. Outwardly it has grown much bigger but inwardly it has been struggling to keep its essential spiritual status. There is none to replace the masters. The spiritual structure of the Ashram is its only *raison d'étre*. The spiritual guidance of Sri Aurobindo and Mother are still there for those who are around them spiritually. How best they can keep the tradition for the posterity depends on them. K. M. Munshi spoke of Sri Aurobindo's influence in making the Ashram atmosphere which continued when he visited and wrote in 1952. Then Mother's influence was working. Now none of them are here. There is certainly a great vacuum. The question of K. M. Munshi hangs in the balance, "How long will this mighty influence last?" (see 'Mother's Homecoming')

Leaving aside other things there is a strong faith and feeling that the Mother is still awake, looking after everything. Though it has its positive and negative sides, the spiritual consciousness around the Samadhi of Sri Aurobindo and the Mother are vibrant, as felt by innumerable devotees and followers of them. If nothing remains, this invisible but ardent faith never fails. We live by her life and teaching.

Notes and References

1. *Mother's Agenda.* Institut de Recherches Evolutives, Paris. 1978. V-1. p.157.
2. *Prayers and Meditations. The Mother. Collected Works.* Pondicherry; Sri Aurobindo Ashram. 1979. V-1. p.81.
3. *Mother's Agenda.* V-2. p.262.
4. "The Mother". *Collected Works of the Mother.* Centenary Edition. 1978. Pondicherry; Sri Aurobindo Ashram. V-11. p.104.

2

Mother's Homecoming

The Mother's came to India for the first time in 1914, met Sri Aurobindo and was convinced that her place of work was here. But the wind of cruel politics tore her away to Europe and Japan. After a long struggle she was able to come back on 24 April 1920 and settle forever in Pondicherry. This was the day of her homecoming.

The ancestry of Mother was Egyptian and Turkish. She was French by birth but Indian by predilection. "O Mother, O soul of India," she said on the occasion of India's independence. India was her mother country.

Barrister Paul Richard first came to Pondicherry in 1910 to campaign for the election of M. Paul Bluyson to the French Chamber of Deputies. He was highly impressed after meeting Sri Aurobindo. Later he spoke and wrote about him very eloquently. After his return Mirra, a great seeker of truth, started communication with the sage of Pondicherry.

In 1914 Paul and Mirra Richards, now married, came to Pondicherry. This time Paul himself was a candidate for the Chamber. Mirra met Sri Aurobindo for the first time at 3-30 pm on 29 March 1914 and received an absolute silence, which she had longed for a long time. At the first meeting she recognized him as the Krishna and Guru of her dream and trance. The spiritual rapport between the two began, and the review, *Arya*, which later contained the major portion of Sri Aurobindo's works, was launched by Richards and Sri Aurobindo, on his birthday on 15 August 1914.

But the Ridhards earned a great disfavour of the British for their association with the most dangerous political refugee,

Aurobindo Ghose and his comrades, including poet Subramania Bharati. The First World War broke out, and the British pressure on the French became mounting to expel political refugees and the Richards from Pondicherry. Though the expulsion of the political refugees to Djibouti could be postponed and later dropped, Richards had to leave for France on 22 February 1915, next day to Mirra's 37th birthday.

She was shocked at first at this expulsion from her spiritual refuge, as sometimes she recorded in her entries in *Prayer and Meditations*. The mental torment continued for some time. She left her soul here, she said.

Paul Richard was given an assignment to visit Japan and China. The Richards reached Yokohama, Japan, on 11 March 1916 and remained there for about four years. While in Japan, Paul Richard wrote a book in French, *Au Japon*, which was translated in English by Madame Mirra Richard. Paul dreamed about the Asian Federation and urged Japan to free Asia from the British domination. When poet Tagore and his party visited Japan, it is reported that Richard tried to register their sympathies for the cause of Asia. He collaborated with the Black Dragon Society whose organ, *Asia Jiron*, honoured Aurobindo Ghose by publishing a flaming article on him with his picture. This society gave shelter to Indian revolutionary leaders like Rashbehari Bose and others. The Richards formed young groups in Japan as earlier in Pondicherry. So they further antagonized the British, whose police reported their passage to Pondicherry, to all the ports of Extreme Orient, as they were sailing back. However, they reached Pondicherry safely on 24 April 1920. It was a day of great relief and high expectation to Madame Mirra Richard.

"It was when the Tapasya for the Siddhi of the Supramental was going on that... the Mother joined Sri Aurobindo intimately in the great spiritual work."[1] wrote A.B. Purani. As earlier, Richards started to live in a separate house. On 24 November of the same year, a cyclonic storm damaged the house where Mirra was living. As a consequence her belongings were shifted to the same house where Sri Aurobindo was living with a limited number of disciples. Gradually she took charge of the household and her caring hands changed its shape. In the course of time Sri Aurobindo introduced her as 'Mother' to his disciples. On 24 November 1926 Lord Krishna descended in Sri Aurobindo. Krishna is Anandamaya, the overhead Godhead preparing the descent of the Supermind, he explained. Mother witnessed the descent. It was marked as the *Siddhi Divas*.

"Then he called everyone, sat in the verandah... had me sit beside him . . . . Then he said, 'I have resolved to withdraw from activity; she will be your Mother and will...' 'he named me officially."[2] The Mother reminisced on 1 April 1970. It was the *de facto* birthday of Sri Aurobindo Ashram. Immersed in *sadhana*, the master never again came out in public. If he was the founder of the ashram the Mother was its real builder. She had a dream that she would create a little world where people would not be dogged by the imperative necessities of life so that they could devote their time for the divine life. The Ashram was the beginning of realizing her dream, she acknowledged later.

The School started in 1943 and was upgraded in 1951. Auroville was founded in 1968. With the expansion of activities the Ashram produced its daily needs. Yoga and study centres were created throughout the country and abroad. Mother communicated with her innumerable children. The Ashramites were 750 in 1952, when K. M. Munshi, the leader and statesman, visited the Ashram. He wrote, "A tennis playing, silk-garmented lady of seventy-five ... saluting the Ashramites at march-past ... yes, the Mother was everywhere. She planned, she financed, she regulated, she drew up schemes of education, buildings and workshops ... she knew every disciple intimately... almost invisible, played such harmonious tunes on this seven-fifty souled orchestra . . . .

"The atmosphere of the Ashram was drawn out of a living and abiding influence... of a man who lived there for nearly four decades . . . . But I ask myself, how long will this mighty influence last?"[3]

About this living influence or the presence of Yogi Sri Aurobindo the Mother related her experience on 17 March

1951, "This precise perception . . . listen, as I had when I came from Japan: I was on the boat, at sea, not expecting anything (I was of course busy with the inner life, but I was living physically on the boat), when all of a sudden, abruptly, about two nautical miles from Pondicherry, the quality, I may even say the physical quality of the atmosphere, of the air, changed so much that I knew we were entering the aura of Sri Aurobindo."[4]

She continued further after a while, "And I can assure you that the area we call 'the Ashram' has a condensation of force which is not at all the same as that of the town, and still less that of the countryside."[5]

"In order to remove many misunderstandings", Sri Aurobindo wrote, "an Asram means the house or houses of a Teacher or Master of spiritual philosophy in which he receives and lodges those who come to him for the teaching and practice . . . and ends with his life-time, unless there is another Teacher who can take his place."[6]

The Mother was the Teacher who took Sri Aurobindo's place and the Ashram reached the pinnacle of its glory during her lifetime. But the question by K. M. Munshi hangs still and we realize the diminishing ray of influence of those who founded and built the body called Ashram, since the departure of Mother in 1973.

Notes and References

1. *The Life of Sri Aurobindo.* Pondicherry; Sri Aurobindo Ashram. 1978. p.211.
2. *Mother's Agenda.* Paris; Institut de Recherches Evolutives. 2000. Vol-11. p.135.
3. Sri Aurobindo Ashram: A Pilgrimage. *The Hindustan Times.* August 15, 1952.
4. *The Mother. Collected Works of the Mother.* Centenary edition. 1978. Pondicherry; Sri Aurobindo Ashram. V-4. p.223.
5. *Ibid.*, p.225.
6. *The Teachings and The Ashram of Sri Aurobindo.* Pondicherry; Sri Aurobindo Ashram.

3

Mother's Image in Her Prayers and Meditations

Prayers and meditations are mostly, as they survive, the records of Mother's entry into a life with Sri Aurobindo to collaborate with his spiritual adventure, an urge to come and settle in Pondicherry.

Mother's prayers, dialogues, realisations and experiences were usually subjective ideas, feelings and aspirations emotionally rendered in the pages of her personal diary. Sometimes they take us to such dizzy, divine heights or compel us to plunge so unfathomably deep inside that it becomes almost impossible to have a total understanding of them. At times we get a glimpse of her personal life. Some of the entries are linked to certain occasions and incidents of her life.

Before her first visit to Pondicherry with Mr. Paul Richard, Madame Mirra Richard wrote in her diary on March 3 1914, "As the day of departure draws near, I enter into a kind of self-communion; I turn with a fond solemnity towards all those thousand little nothings around us which have silently, for so many years, played their role of faithful friends; I thank them gratefully for all the charm they were able to give . . . I wish that if they are destined to pass into other hands . . . these hands may be gentle to them and know all the respect that is due. . . .

"Then I turn towards the future . . . outer circumstances have no importance at all; my only wish is that this may be for us the beginning of a new inner period . . . may he a period of greater light, greater love, of a more perfect dedication to Thy cause." (*P and M*).

Next day she wrote, "It is likely to be the last time for a long while that I am writing at this table, in this calm room all charged with Thy presence . . . . In an indrawn state I contemplate this turning page, vanishing into the dream of the future and look at the new page all full potentially of the dream of the future . . ." (*P and M*).

Hope and aspiration was rising in her heart. She became conscious of her mission as she sailed on board the Kaga Maru. She felt a change of atmosphere. On March 24 1914 she prayed to God, Grant that I may accomplish my mission, that I may help in Thy integral manifestation. (*P and M*)

On March 29 March 1914 Mirra met Sri Aubobindo for the first time. Next day she wrote in her diary, "In the presence of those who are integrally Thy servitors, those who have attained the perfect consciousness of Thy presence, I become aware that I am still far, very far from what I yearn to realize. . ." (*P and M*)

But far from being depressed, her energy, aspiration and convictions were greatly strengthened. She wrote after one more chapter, "It matters little that there are thousands of beings plunged in the densest ignorance, He whom we saw yesterday is on earth; His presence is enough to prove that a day will come when darkness shall be transformed into light, and Thy reign shall be indeed established upon earth."

Mirra wished to remain in Pondicherry but the First World War broke out, and for some compelling reasons she had to leave Pondicherry on 22 February 1915. While returning to Europe on hoard the Japanese ship *Kamo Maru*, she wrote on 4 March 1915, "Each turn of the propeller upon the deep ocean seems to drag me farther away from my true destiny, the one best expressing the divine will; each passing hour seems to plunge me again deeper into that past with which I had broken, sure of being called to new and vaster realisations; everything seems to draw me back to a state of things totally contrary to the life of my soul which reigns uncontested over outer activities . ." (*P and M*)

"I am exiled from every spiritual happiness, and of all ordeals this, OLord, is surely the most painful that Thou canst impose . . .

"But it refuses to despair, it refuses to believe that the misfortune is irreparable," she wrote on 7 March 1915." (*P and M*)

As she was taken away from her predilected country, her spiritual abode, away from the presence of Sri Aurobindo, she fell very sick. Her diary note of 19 April 1915 reveals, "All external circumstances have changed, giving a flat lie to the dream of the ideal which sought expression even in material activities . . ." The physical being is plunged once again into the dull, monotonous night from which it wanted to withdraw. . ." (*P and M*)

Back home in Paris, old memories confronted her. On November 2 1915 she wrote, "As a strong breeze passes over the sea and crowns with foam its countless waves, so a great breath passed over the memory and awoke the multitude of its remembrances. Intense, complex, crowded, the past lived again in a flash, having lost nothing of its savour, its richness." (*P and M*)

Her whole being surged up in a flood of gratitude and adoration. Gathering all her memories like an abundant harvest she offered them at the feet of the Lord. The First World War had been raging throughout Europe, and she had had some agonizing experiences of air-raids and trench warfare. Some of the entries at this time depict her mind in turmoil: "For the last two days the earth seems to have been going through a decisive crisis; it seems that the great formidable contest between material resistences and spiritual powers is nearing its conclusion or, in any case, that some element of capital importance has made or is going to make its appearance in the play.

"How little do individual beings count at such times! They are like wisps of straw carried away by the passing breeze . . . to be flung back upon it again and reduced to dust." (*P and M*; 7 November 1915)

She did not remain there for long. She went to England and then to Japan. She reached Tokyo on March 13 1916. Her acquaintance with Japan was splendid at the beginning. She loved the picturesque landscape, Mount Fuji, the tea ceremony, the flower arrangement—all the special features of Japan. The vitally strong, artistic and deeply cultured people of Japan moved her. She began collecting some fine paintings and busied herself with painting, teaching French and learning Japanese. She was even engaged in occult practices, attended lectures and delivered some herself. But still she was not happy, and often fell ill. She was compelled to stay put in Japan, for reasons beyond her control. Her soul remained at Pondicherry. All seemed meaningless. She felt as if she had been plunged into commonplace situations, forced to live among common people with common desires, banished from the spiritual poise and divine savour. She sighed and raised a thousand questions but ultimately that infinite hope persisted. Forever an optimist, she never lost her conviction. For a long time there was no entry in her diary. Maybe it was a long silence of preparation. It may also be that many entries did not survive the test of selection for her book, *Prayers and Meditations.* However, a few entries, from her diary during her stay in Japan may throw some light on the situation.

"Lord, I could in truth say that I have neither yoga nor virtues, for I am completely divested of that which constitutes the glory of all those who want to serve Thee." (*P and M*; 7 December 1916)

"I was spoiled by Thee formerly: Thou madest me live so constantly in Thy Presence . . . . But now it seems that Thou wouldst teach me to know the unchanging bliss even in darkness, and not to have any preference for either consciousness or unconsciousness." (*P and M*; 10 December I 916)

Her condition may be better realised from her note on 28 November 1916 (*P and M*) where she compared herself to a bird without shackle, yet not able to fly in the sky: "Conscious of its freedom, it does not enjoy it, and remains like the others, among the others, perched on the ground in the midst of the dark and dense fog."

She had many dialogues with the divine, as per her notes, which are replete with pertinent questions. Sometimes she felt deprived of all the opportunities. Sometimes she felt that she had been given the opportunity of living amongst the ordinary people with many imperfections so that she might learn to realise the divine under such trying circumstances. Not only personal affairs, events in the contemporary world also were recorded in her diary. Her reflections on the First World War were mentioned on many occasions. She felt that individuals had no value in such matters, however much their importance might be according to historians. This idea resembles that of Tolstoy, the great novelist, as we find in his *War and Peace.* Mother wrote on 7 November 1915, "Matter, tortured, takes shelter at Thy feet, its last and only refuge . . . . O Lord of Truth, this individual world blesses Thy truth which it does not yet know, but which it calls, and to which it adheres with all the joyful energy of its living forces."

Amidst the horror of the war, in spite of her personal difficulties and problems, Mother never lost hope about reaching the goal of divine realisation and about man and the earth. She wanted to be the incarnation of Divine Love, remain a love-link between God and man. "Thou knowest what happiness would be mine if by Thy grace I could be integrally transformed into a hearth of divine love - that love which is the first and highest manifestation of Thy eternal Truth, that love which is at once the completest expression in this world of Thy Truth and the most direct road to lead to it the human consciousness that has gone astray," she wrote on 21 December 1916 (*P and M*). She experienced this divine love in herself, "Thou gavest me this evening a foretaste of what Thou expectest from me, only a foretaste . . . it was the heart which thus overflowed under the pressure of the powers of love Thou didst pour into it, and the whole being began to love, to love ever more and more, without any definite aim," she felt on 24 December 1916. (*P and M*)

She heard in the silence and noted the command of God, the next day," Be this love in all things and everywhere, ever more widely, ever more intensely, and the whole world will become at the same time Thy work and Thy wealth, Thy field of action and Thy conquest. Fight persistently to break down the last limits which are only frail barriers before the expansion of the being . . . . Fight in order to conquer and triumph; fight to overcome everything that was till today, to make the New Light spring forth, the New Example the world needs. Fight stubbornly against all obstacles, inner or outer. It is the pearl of great price which is offered for thy Realisation." (*P and M*) For considerable times before and after her return to her destined place Pondicherry, very few entries were made in her diary; two in 1918 and one each in 1919, 1920, 1927, 1928, 1931 and 1937. The first part of her diary ended in 1919, before her permanent settlement in Pondicherry. The second part comprises of five entries only. She wrote her diary in French, and a few of the entries were translated by Sri Aurobindo himself. Some examples of Mother's meditations as on May 6, 1927 (*P and M*):

"One must know how to give one's life and also one's death, give one's happiness and also one's suffering, to depend for everything and in all things upon the Divine Dispenser . . . who alone can and will decide whether we shall be happy or not, whether we shall live or not, whether we shall participate or not in the realisation.

"In the integrality and absoluteness of this love, this self-giving, lies the essential condition for perfect peace, the indispensable foundation of constant beatitude."

"There is a Power that no ruler can command; there is a Happiness that no earthly success can bring; there is a Light that no wisdom can possess; there is a Knowledge that no philosophy and no science can master; there is a Bliss of which no satisfaction of desire can give the enjoyment; there is a thirst for Love that no human relation can appease; there is a Peace that one finds nowhere, not even in death. It is the Power, the Happiness, the Light, the Knowledge, the Bliss, the Love, the Peace that flow from the Divine Grace." (*P and M*; December 28, 1928)

Work Cited

Prayers and Meditations. The Mother. Centenary Edition. Pondicherry; Sri Aurobindo Ashram. Vol-1 and also a separate book on the subject.

4

Our Earthly Mother and Her Divine Self

The Mother once said, "Since the Beginning of the earth, whenever and wherever there was the possibility of manifesting a ray of consciousness, I was there." Then, on 14 February 1973 she said, "I am nearing my hundredth year—it's only five Years away—and I started my effort to become conscious when I was five. It's a fact. . . . Now, of course, I have come to doing the work in the cells of the body, but the work started long ago."[1]

The Mother had been spearheading the rise of Consciousness from the inconscient, organising the evolution of consciousness from her births immemorial; from the beginning of the earth and surely in this life too. She had been engaged in the same work almost from the beginning of her this mortal birth. Sri Aurobindo said that Mother, who had been conscious from a very early age, had the same goal of Transformation as Sri Aurobindo's even before she met him. And about her identity he clarified the point in reply to a disciple's question:

"The Divine puts on an appearance of humanity, assumes the outward human nature in order to tread the path and show it to human beings, but does not cease to be the Divine. It is a manifestation . . . of a growing divine Consciousness, not human turning into divine. The Mother was inwardly above the human even in childhood, so the view held by 'many' is erroneous."[2]

The Divine Mother was growing conscious of herself from the age of five. From her childhood she would go deep within during her meditation, under the old trees of Fontainbleu. Afterward she started recording her personal dialogues with the Divine (Le Seigneur) in her notebooks from the beginning of 1912. She would sit before an open window at 5 in the morning with a shawl wrapped round her shoulders during the winter. Just after the meditation she would record her experiences in her notebook and keep the same in a drawer under lock and key. Gradually the notes became few and far between. The book was titled *Pri`eres et Meditations de la M`ere*. The selected few, which were translated by Sri Aurobindo himself, were published in 1962 in a book titled *Prayers and Meditations.*

Mother edited them drastically and only those surviving the test were published. The remaining portion were of the Diaries as destroyed. Today nothing except those prayers, which survive in the pages of the book, are available. The book is considered to be the best of Mother's literary Jewels presented to her children. The Rishis, seer poets of the *Vedas*, had seen and heard what they produced as *Suktas*, as such the other name of the *Veda* is 'Shruti'. In that sense we may call *Prayers and Meditations* also 'Shruti'. She too had seen and heard, had dialogues with the Divine. Sri Aurobindo, in reply to one of his disciples, wrote on 21. 8. 1936:

"The prayers are mostly written in an identification with the earth consciousness. It is the Mother in the lower nature addressing the Mother in her higher nature .... It is the Divine who is always referred to as Divin Ma`itre and Seigneur. There is the Mother who is carrying on the Sadhana and the Divine Mother, both being one but in different poises, and both turn to the Seigneur or Divine Master. This kind of prayers from the Divine to the Divine you will find also in the *Ramayana* and the *Mahabharata*."[3]

Let us go through a few of her notes to realise the Mother in relation to her divine self.

"I shall no more have anything to say to Thee, for then I shall be Thou. This is the goal that I would reach; towards this victory all my efforts will tend more and more. I aspire for the day when I can no longer say 'I' for! I shall be Thou." (2.11.1912)

"All my thoughts go towards Thee, all my acts are consecrated to Thee; Thy presence is for me an absolute, immutable, invariable fact, and Thy peace dwells constantly in my heart. Yet I know that this state of Union is poor and precarious compared with that which it will become possible for me to realise tomorrow, and I am as yet far, no doubt very far, from that identification in which I shall totally lose the notion of the 'I', of that 'I', which I still use in order to express myself, but which is each time a constraint, like a term unfit to express the thought that is seeking for expression." (19.11.1912)

"When Thou wiliest I shall be in Thee, Thyself, and there shall be no more any distinction; I await that blessed hour without impatience of any kind, letting myself flow irresistibly toward it as a peaceful stream flows toward the boundless ocean." (7.12.1912)

"I await without haste, without inquietude, the tearing of another veil, the union made complete. I know that the veil is formed of a whole mass of small imperfections, of attachments without number . . . . How shall all these disappear?" (11.12.1912)

"My progress is slow, very slow, but I hope that in compensation it may be lasting and free from all fluctuation. "Grant that I may accomplish my mission, that I may help in Thy integral manifestation." (24.3.1914)

"It seems to me that I am being born to a new life and all the methods, the habits of the past can no longer be of any use . . . . I feel as though 1 have done nothing yet, as though I have not lived a spiritual life, only entered the path that leads to it, it seems to me that I know nothing . . . . It is as though I were stripped of my entire past . . . as though all that has vanished and made room for a newborn child whose whole existence is yet to be lived" (3.4.1914)

"Lord, Thou hast answered my prayer, Thou hast granted me what I have asked from Thee; the '1' has disappeared, there is only a docile instrument put at Thy service, a centre of concentration and manifestation of thy infinite and external ways; Thou hast taken my life and made it Thine . . . ." (10.4.1914).

"O Lord, O my sweet Master, sole Reality, dispel this feeling of the '1'. 1 have now understood that so long as there will be a manifested universe, the 'I' will remain necessary for Thy manifestation; to dissolve, or even to diminish or weaken the 'I', is to deprive Thee of the means of manifestation, in whole or part. But what must be radically and definitively suppressed is the illusory feeling, the illusory sensation of the separate 'I'. At no moment, in no circumstances must we forget that our 'I' has no reality outside Thee." (17.4.1914)

"Thou hast taken entire possession of this miserable instrument and if it is not yet perfected enough for Thee to complete its transformation, its transmutation, Thou art at work in each one of its cells . . . ." (22.1.1916)

"Once more Thou hast taken me in Thy omnipotent arms and cradled me on Thy unfathomable heart, and Thy heart said to me, 'Torment not thyself at all, be confident like a child; art thou not myself crystallised for my work?" (26.12.1916)

These all are the earthly Mother's subjective reflections, like a tête-a-tête with her Divine self. We can very well find how the 'I' of the Mother was undergoing a different, altogether fresh experience now and going back to an apparent old position again. Her 'I' was getting dissolved and again rising up with a new explanation. One 'I' was merging with the other 'I' and again separating itself. Sri Ramakrishna considered this question of 'I' in various ways. He described how Hanuman, Narada and Sankaracharya, after having realised the Lord in their different ways, retained the ego of a servant, of a knower and of a preceptor respectively. So Sri Ramakrishna said that one may reason it away for a time but it comes up again. One cannot rid oneself of the ego which says, 'I','I' for the ego is like a water-jar and the absolute is the shoreless ocean in which the water-jar is merged. You may reason that the infinite or the absolute is both within and without; but you cannot shake yourself free of the water-jar so long as you reason. The so-called absolute is something relative to you so long as you reason. This water-jar that you cannot shake off is the self or ego of divine love. So long as there is the water-jar or ego, there are both 'I' and 'Thou'. Thus, "Thou are the Lord, I am the servant of the Lord."

In his epic poem *Savitri* (Book Three, Canto II) Sri Aurobindo speaks of the Divine Mother:

Across the silence of the ultimate calm,
Out of a marvellous Transcendence' core,
A body of wonder and translucency
As if a sweet mystic summary of her self
Escaping into the original Bliss
Had come enlarged out of eternity,
Someone came infinite and absolute.
A being of wisdom, power and delight,
Even as a Mother draws her child to her arms,
Took to her breast Nature and world and soul.[4]

And the Mother had recorded, "Many a time in the day and night it seems to me that I am, or rather my consciousness is, concentrated entirely in my heart which is no longer an organ, not even a feeling, but the divine Love, impersonal, eternal; and living this Love I feel myself living at the centre of each thing upon the entire earth, and at the same time I seem to stretch out immense, infinite arms and envelop with a boundless tenderness all beings, clasped, gathered, nestled on my breast that is vaster than the universe." (22.2.1914)

Earlier, Mother recorded a sweet memory of hers when she was a child of 13. Every night she would dream herself going up and up, very high above out of the body, clad in a golden robe. All suffering, miserable people of all ages would come under the fold of her extended robe, and whoever happened to touch the robe would be relieved of all miseries and would return home happily. The dream continued for a year and the child would cherish this nocturnal experience more than anything else among her daily activities. This the poet of *Savitri* (BookThree, Canto II) envisioned thus:

All nature dumbly calls to her alone
To heal with her feet the aching throb of life
And break the seals on the dim soul of man
And kindle her fire in the closed heart of things.[5]

"The heavens are definitely conquered, and nothing and nobody could have the power of wresting them from me. But the conquest of the earth is still to be made; it is being carried on in the very heart of the turmoil" (*Prayers and Meditations*: 31.7.1915). This conquest of the earth was the crux of the matter, the Core of the Sadhana, the Supermental yoga of Mother and Sri Aurobindo. Sri Aurobindo had the goal of not getting dissolved in the heavens but bringing down the heaven itself into the earth nature so that our mundane life may become a 'Life Divine'. To be precise, Sri Aurobindo brought down on his body the 'Mind of Light', Supramental light and force but it did not get the time to transform the physical. As he left his body his light and force supramentalised the body of the Mother. "To transform each cell of her body, enlighten them, was her Sadhana. She had immense hope and, expectations: The physical body . . . . one day it will be capable of building a bridge between the physical life as we know it and the suprarnental life which is to manifest."[6]

She tried to make her body a bridge and it served her most — to the extent possible. Her attitude was — "We live only because Thou willest it. We do not die unless Thou willest it." (from *Champaidal's Treasures*. p.86). She was there from the beginning of the earth. She will continue to remain throughout the existence. She indeed once told Nolini Kanta Gupta, "If ever I leave my body my consciousness shall remain with you."

Notes and References

1. *Mother's Agenda*. Satprem. Paris; Institut de Recherches Evolutives. 1983. V-13. p. 363.
2. Sri Aurobindo. *The Mother*. Pondicherry; SABCL, Sri Aurobindo Ashram. 1972. V-25. p.48.
3. *Prayers and Meditations. The Mother. Collected Works*; Centenary Edition. Pondicherry; Sri Aurobindo Ashram. V-1. p.379.
4. Sri Aurobindo. *Savitri. Collected Works*. Pondicherry; SABCL, Sri Aurobindo Ashram. V-28. p.312.
5. *Savitri*. p.314.
6. *On Thoughts and Aphorisms* (No. 11). *The Mother*. Collected Works. Centenary Edition. Pondicherry; Sri Aurobindo Ashram. 1978. V-10. pp. 31-32

Work Cited

Prayers and Meditations. The Mother. Collected Works; Centenary Edition. Pondicherry; Sri Aurobindo Ashram. V-1.

5

Mother of Animals

The carnivores eat flesh of each other. Men are no exceptions to this practice. They too eat the flesh of other animals. Men were cannibals once. They may still do it in some parts of the world. Before speaking about Mother on the subject it might be pertinent to refresh our memory about the man-animal relationship.

Man with his mental abilities is superior to other living beings. Yet he remains an animal in many ways. In fact, man can be infinitely crueler than animals. Absence of empathy may be the main cause for such cruelty. Charles Darwin described an incident of cannibalism at Tiera Del Fuego, during a voyage in 1932. They observed that men ate the older women of their family, when pressed by hunger during the winter. They singed them in the fire and ate them before they thought of killing their dogs because the dogs could catch the otters but the old women could not. He also recorded his observation that in Las Vacas people practised extreme cruelty on the horses merely for petty gain, to show their heroism, or to entertain themselves.

During the first quarter of this century the Prince of Wales visited the kingdom of Sirpur. Gita Mehta, in her novel *Raj,* described how loyal kings and princes used to entertain their royal guests. To help the royal party to hunt the tigers easily, the beasts were caught beforehand, drugged and kept in the cages with big bricks hanging on the end of their tails. Then they were released into the jungle to be killed. And there were competitions among them. To upstage the efforts of Jaipur in showing elephant fights, Udaipur set 300 leopards to fight 300 wild boars for the entertainment of the Prince. In Bikaner the royal party killed 11,000 grouse in one day. They jokingly said that Bikaner was made by the god of grouse. Tiger meat is a delicacy in Taiwan. In China parts of a tiger's body are in great demand for their aphrodisiac value. Hence it has become an endangered species.

Mother had a very tender heart with the universal Mother's love and affection for all her children: human and animal. From her notes in *Prayers and Meditations* dated 2 February 1914 we know: "Many a time it seems to me that I am, or rather my consciousness is, concentrated entirely in my heart which is no longer an organ, not even a feeling, but the divine Love, impersonal, eternal; and being this Love I feel myself living at the centre of each thing upon the entire earth and at the same time I seem to stretch out immense, infinite arms and envelop with a boundless tenderness all beings, clasped, gathered, nestled on my breast that is vaster than the universe."

From the age of 12 Mirra would walk into the neighbouring woods at Fontainbleau near her house in Paris. She would sit under a very big tree, leaning against its trunk for hours, deep in communion with the infinitude and with primordial nature. Some of the trees were 2,000 year old. Squirrels would lovingly crawl over her, birds would perch on her. On opening her eyes she would find a deer looking at her. Sometimes a big tree, decreed by woodcutters to be cut down, would approach her imploring to be saved. Sometimes the tree was really saved from the murderous axe due to her intervention. Her companionship with nature was a very genuine one. She felt a spiritual oneness with all life, all nature.

Mirra bad her own way of dealing with things. She always stood with a calm understanding before any action. She sometimes visited the parks with her father. Here is one of her childhood stories: "In Paris, there is a park called the 'Jardin des Plantes', where there are animals as well as plantes. A magnificent lion had just been received there. Naturally, he was caged. And he was furious. In his cage was a door, behind which he could hide. And sure enough, whenever visitors came to see him, he would go hide himself. I had observed this; so one day, I stood near the cage and began speaking to him—animals are very sensitive to articulate language, they really listen. I started speaking gently to my lion. I said to him; 'Oh, how beautiful you are! What a pity you hide thus, we would so much love to see you'. . . . Well, he was listening. Then, little by little, he cocked an eye at me . . . next he stretched his limbs and finally pressed his nose on the bar with an air as though to say, "At long last, here is someone who understands me!"[1]

In 1906 she went to Tlemcen in Algeria to learn and practise occultism from Max and Madam Theon. Miracles happened there regularly and Mirra had shown enough capacity to master the occult science. She later related the story of a dog there. The dog belonged to Theon. It was a big dog but was fondly called 'Little Boy'.

"A dog that could exteriorize! It would dream and go out of its body! This dog had a kind of adoration for me. I should mention that at a fixed time in the afternoon I always went into a trance—I had meditation followed by trance. When it was over I would go out walking with Theon and the dog always came with us; he usually came to fetch me in my room. One day I was lying on a divan, in a trance, when I felt his cold nose thrust into my hand in order to wake me up. I open my eyes . . . no dog. Yet I had positively, distinctly felt his cold nose muzzling my hand to wake me up. Well, I got ready, went down the stairs, and who did I find on the landing? My dog, in a deep slumber, he too in a state of trance! He had come to me in his sleep to wake me up . . . . he woke up, gave himself a shake and trotted off."[2]

Mother loved her two dogs, Goro and Puchi. We have her photograph with them in Japan, taken some time around 1918. She had another admirer in Tlemcen, a big warty toad. Whenever Mirra played her piano, it would hop over and listen rapturously with bulging eyes, and the moment the music ended, it would go away. She even had some strange encounters with snakes. In her own words:

"There were centuries old olive trees in Theon's estate. I would sit under one of them every day at noon to meditate. Yes, it was hot at high noon, but the heat never bothered me. Quite the contrary. Now, one day, I was deep in my meditation when

I began to feel uneasy. So then I open my eyes. And what do I see? About two meters away in front of me, standing erect and swaying its hood, is a Naja, hissing furiously at me. You know 'Naja'? They are like Nagas here, the Hooded cobra and extremely poisonous! Their poison is deadly . . . . At first I didn't understand why the serpent was so enraged. Then I remembered that just behind me there was a hole in the tree. 'I must be sitting here barring its way to its hole', I thought. 'But what's to be done now?' I was in quandary. Any movement, be it ever so light, would instantly make it strike me. Mark you, I didn't feel any fear. I just sat still and stared fixedly at its eyes and exerted my will force to the utmost. Gradually the hissing softened, then stopped altogether. After sometime, slowly, very slowly I drew away my legs, first one then the other. But all the while I kept my stare fixed on it and steadily exerted my will. At last the venomous snake suddenly lowered is hood, and quickly turning round slithered into the nearby pool."[3]

"After this incident there was another, when I helped a cat to defeat a little asp . . . . The cat was a big russet angora, who, at first, began playing with the asp, then, of course, became furious. The asp kept jumping at him and the cat—it was extraordinary, I watched this for over ten minutes—the cat leapt aside so swiftly that the asp just missed him. And as it darted by, the cat struck at it with all his claws out, scratching it each time. The other lost its energy little by little. And at the end. . . I stopped the cat from eating it, for it was sickening."[4]

After she had settled in Pondicherry Mother had another encounter with a snake. Years later she would recall: "Long ago, 1 often used to take a drive and then get down somewhere and walk. One day after my walk, I got back into the car and was just about to drive away. The door was still open when, exactly from the spot I had just left, a fairly large snake came out. It was furious. Belligerently it came and headed straight towards the open door, ready to spring at me. Luckily I was alone, neither the driver nor Pavitra were there, otherwise . . . . The snake came on and when it had come quite near, I looked closely at it and said, 'What do you want? Why have you come here?'

"There was a pause. Then it fell down flat and was gone. You know, they have a way of suddenly falling down, going limp, and prrt! gone!"[5]

In the course of her divine ministry Mother had ample scope to know this creature well. To a question a like what does the serpent represent, Mother replied that it is a vibration of evolution; materially it is a tremendous concentration of vitality, a progressive energy of motion. And to a question, why does the animal always give us this evil feeling, she said that it was mere incomprehension.

Stepping into the realm of the occult, where Mirra had free access, we come to know that she had met the king of cats and serpents who were the heads of their respective species. While the cat-king conferred on her the power over his species, the serpent-king came to make an understanding with her that in return for the promise that serpents would not do her any harm, she would never kill them. But Mirra could not agree to the proposal. Although she had no ill-feeling towards the snakes, she would have to protect her dependents in case any of them were attacked by a snake. She did not commit herself. The matter ended there.

Mother had known many kinds of animals but she loved cats the most. In one of her talks, on 8 January 1951 she said, "I have studied cats a lot; if one knows them well, they are marvellous creatures."[6] She had a great storehouse of lively anecdotes which she would relate to a spellbound audience from time to time.

One of the early inmates of the Ashram, Kanai Lal Ganguly, recalls from his memory that Mother had two cats on her shoulders and he found few more as he looked around. One of the cats from her shoulder jumped on Sri Aurobindo's throne chair. Another old disciple remembered that in the early days of the Ashram, Mother used to prepare the pudding herself and would often put a little aside. After mixing some milk she would stir it a little. It was for her cats.

Mother had many cats staying with her, named Bushy, Kiki, Sundari, etc. During her conversation on 22 March 1951 she told the story of her extraordinary cat Kiki: "I had a very sweet little cat, absolutely civilised, a marvellous cat. It was born in the house and it had the habit all cats have, that is to say, if something moved, it played with that. Just then there was in the house a huge scorpion. It started playing with the scorpion. And the scorpion stung it. But it was an exceptional cat; it came to me, it was almost dying, but it showed me its paw where it was bitten—it was already swollen and in a terrible state. I took my little cat—it was really sweet—and put it on a table and called Sri Aurobindo. I told him, 'Kiki has been stung by a scorpion, it must be cured.' The cat stretched its neck and looked at Sri Aurobindo, its eyes already a little glassy. Sri Aurobindo sat before it and looked at it also. Then we saw this little cat gradually beginning to recover, to come round, and an hour later it jumped to its feet and went away, completely healed. . . ."

In those days she meditated with her disciples. Every time Kiki would occupy a particular chair before the session commenced and would remain in trance for hours together, much beyond the others. At such times it refused even food. Bushy, another of Mother's cats, used to pick up all her kittens with her teeth, one by one, and drop them at Mother's feet as soon as they were old enough to see, as an offering to her. In so doing, the cat must have felt fully secured and free from danger.

Another of Mother's cat-experiences:

"I have known mother-cats which have sacrificed themselves entirely for their babies—people speak of maternal love *with* such admiration, as though its were purely a human privilege, but I have seen this love manifested by mother-cats to a degree far surpassing humanity. I have seen a mother-cat which would never touch her food until her babies had taken all they needed. I have seen another cat which stayed for eight long days beside her kittens, without satisfying any of her needs, because she was afraid to leave them alone; then again, there was a cat which repeated the same movement more than fifty times to teach her young one how to jump from a wall on to a window, and I may add, with care, intelligence and skill which many uneducated woman would not have."[7]

Some more eerie incidents about cats which occurred quite a long time ago in France as she relates. This one happened before the First World War. During those days Mirra Alfassa used to have small meetings with three or four intellectuals in her house in Paris on every Wednesday evening. One of them was a light-hearted poet, a boy who attended every meeting. On one such occasion he was missing, which was unusual. Specially because a few days earlier he had promised to come on that particular day. Meeting over, Mirra opened the door to let the others go out. And there, before the door, sat a big, dark grey cat. It rushed into the room and jumped upon her mewing desperately. She looked into its eyes and told herself— "Well, these are so-and-so's eyes . . . . Surely something has happened to him." And the next morning . . . he was found lying strangled on his bed.

The other story is about a boy who was a poet and an artist. He had gone to the war during the First World War. Mirra liked him so much that his photograph was framed and hung in her room. His letters arrived from time to time but information about him was reaching very irregularly. There was no news for some days. "One day" said Mother, "I came into my room, and the moment I entered, the photograph crashed down from the wall where it had been well-fixed, and the glass shattered to pieces. I felt a little anxious, I said, 'There is something wrong.' But we had no news. Two or three days later ... I opened the entrance door and a big grey cat rushed in - light grey this time - a magnificent cat, and just as the other one had done, it flung itself upon me, ... mewing. I looked into its eyes — it had the eyes of that boy. And this cat, it kept on circling around me and all the time tugged at my dress and miaowed. I wanted to put it out, but it would not go .... The next day it was announced in the papers, that this boy had been found dead between two trenches, dead for three days. That is, he must have died at the time when his photograph had fallen ... cats live in the vital world, they have a very developed vital consciousness and can easily be taken possession of by vital forces."[8]

Talking about the human perversion she once related the story of a monkey.

"There is a story about some officers in North Africa—in Algeria—who had adopted a monkey. The monkey lived with them and one day at dinner they had a grotesque idea and gave the monkey some alcohol to drink. The monkey first saw the others drink, this seemed to it something quite interesting, and it drank a glass, a full glass of wine. Afterwards it was ill, as ill as could be: it rolled under the table with all kinds of pains and was really in a very bad way, that is, it gave the men an example of the spontaneous effect of alcohol when the physical nature is not already perverted. It nearly died of poisoning. But it finally recovered. And some time later it was again allowed to come for dinner as it was all right, and somebody placed a glass of wine in front of it. It picked it up in a terrible rage and flung it back at the head of the man . . . . By that it showed that it was much wiser than the man!"[9]

Now we come to the story of her relation with some other domestic animals. Sri Aurobindo had come to Pondicherry in 1910. Mirra finally settled in Pondicherry in 1920, as a collaborator of the Yogi. With the passage of time the number of disciples increased. When Sri Aurobindo went into seclusion in 1926 for spiritual purposes, she was given the charge of the establishment, that gradually came to be known as Sri Aurobindo Ashram. Sri Aurobindo himself named her Mother. In course of time, Mirra become Mother of her innumerable children throughout the world. With the human inmates, a few animals also became members of the establishment. Cats were already there. Now two bullocks were purchased by the Ashram for ploughing the fields. They were named Ojas and Tej. Even a sparrow nesting in the house was taken care of by Sri Aurobindo and Mother. It is no wonder that Mother framed rules about the living conditions, the working hours and the recess hours of the animals. Sri Aurobindo also shared the job. To Mother, the non-human part of creation was no less important than the human part. She ordered that proper diet should be given to the animals. Food served to them was to be clean and in right proportions. She was very concerned about cruelty to the animals which she never permitted. There are some extracts from the correspondences of Sri Aurobindo and Mother in this respect:

Sri Aurobindo on 4. 3. 1932: The Mother is quite against the system of boring the nose of the bullocks. Are they so wild that it is thought necessary to do this to tame them? Then again, a month later, You had promised that the bullocks would not be beaten, but we have been told by more than one eye-witness that they have been beaten by yourself and the servants, and badly beaten too. We strongly disapprove, we are entirely against this kind of maltreatment. It is not by beating but by patience and persistent will, without getting into a nervous irritation, that work can be taught to animals. They are far more intelligent than you believe. And again, It was seen by others that Tej received not one but eight or nine blows and there was swelling and marks afterwards. You will tell the man that if this happens again he will be dismissed. I had said that if the bullocks showed unwillingness the chaki work has to be stopped. Please understand that I mean it.

Mother wrote on 14. 9. 1932, "I have watched the incident from the roof, and saw with inner sight too. The bullocks are not mischievous. One the contrary, they are very good and peaceful creatures, but very sensitive—unusually sensitive perhaps . . . . . The truth is that they dislike and distrust the present driver, and not without reason . . . . I see no solution but to change the man and to find a better one. The proposal to frighten them in order to master them is unacceptable . . . . The beasts lose more and more confidence and joy and peace and finally their strength and even their health goes.

"What is the use of being a sadhak if, as soon as we act, we act like the ignorant ordinary man?

"From the roof I concentrated the power on the bullocks ordering them to yield and obey and found them quite receptive. To use a quiet, steady, unwavering conscious will, that is the way, the only true way really effective and worthy of an aspirant of Divine life.

"I object strongly to his way of twisting the tails of the beasts. If somebody twisted one of his limbs like that what would he say? And I am pretty sure that our bullocks are more sensitive than he is."

Someone reported that a cow did not take food from the feeding tub as desired, for which the cow had been beaten on its head by a sandal. Hearing the report, Mother said that it was an action both brutal and stupid. It would only manage to make the cow vindictive and violent. A bullock was steadily losing weight. Mother observed it and wrote on 1 February 1934 that a doctor should be consulted and it is better that the bullock remains without work and is allowed to move freely in the pasture for some time for there is no better cure than the open air and sun.

A boy had hurt a dog while rashly dragging a cart. He was dismissed from service by the order of the Mother and she never permitted him to be reemployed even for a temporary period. She said that the boy had almost willingly hurt the dog. And it was very likely that he would hurt the cow and the calf. She did not approve of engaging animals in the circus, to be tortured for man's amusement and earning. She did not approve of going to the circus and said so when one of her disciples asked for her permission. One of her remarks on the man-animal relationship:

"I have seen in animals all the reactions, emotional, affective, sentimental, all the feelings of which men are so proud. The only difference is that animals can not speak of them and write about them, so we consider them inferior beings because they can not flood us with books on what they have felt.

Once Mother saw a washerman's donkey passing through the road with its young one—a common sight in those days. Seeing her intently looking at them, Udar Pinto, one of the disciples, offered to purchase the colt for the Mother if she agreed. She consented. The colt began its life anew with Udar and his family, in their garden. Its friends were the dogs. They played together. Mother fondly called it Baudet.

In 1946, Richard Pearson, an eleven-year old boy, came to live in the Ashram with his father. Leaving him with the Pintos, his father left for Madras to rejoin his Army unit. The boy fell in love with the colt. When Udar's family shifted to another house within a few months, the animal got a shelter at Jalad's Dairy. At this point of time Richard approached the Mother to be given charge of the animal. She agreed.

Both the human and non-human children were growing up under Mother's keen eyes. Richard used to bring the animal under Mother's balcony, daily at 6-15 am, when other sadhaks also reached there to receive a touch of Mother's divine blessings. The colt used to be brought on Sundays too at 4-30 pm to join the assembly of some 30 or more cows under her balcony. The first was called the Balcony Darshan and the latter one was called the Cow Darshan. Richard used to go up to the end of the beach road along the sea every morning, riding the colt. At noon he took the colt to the Ashram Dining Room to bring breadcrumbs for it. The colt took fodder too, like the cows. Richard brushed and bathed the colt. The colt had seen less of its species than dogs and cows. It never kicked and wanted to play with the cows but the latter did not like it. In the course of time it was allotted a separate shed to live in as it was not liked by the cows.

Unlike the common belief, the donkey grew up to be quite intelligent but it was very obstinate and not at all amenable to work. It learnt to run like a dog and would often run away. It was a tough job for Richard to manage it. Naturally, he used to lose his temper and beat up the animal at times.

Really he loved the colt. The two became famous. But he was called the donkey-boy by the town people. A few years passed by. Both of them grew up. Richard busied himself in his studies. Gradually he had lesser time to be with the animal. Perhaps it lived for another ten years and then it was lost. No one knew what happened to it.

As Richard was remembering on his boyhood days, Baudet was crowned. Krishnalal made a painting of the crowned colt. His eyes suddenly flashed. He vividly remembered the donkey race that took place in Pondicherry. He was one of the competitors. It was held on 14 July 1948. Some six donkeys with their riders gathered together on the promenade. There was a large crowd on the beach, gathered to see the fun. Baudet was so excited that it ventured to push and run ahead of others before time. But when the gun was fired, it would not move. Other donkeys were very slow in their movement but one of them moved ahead. When it had almost reached the end of the track Baudet ran and overtook it. But reaching the first runner the two started walking as if there was no need to compete. The crowd pushed and jolted. Someone tried to pull Baudet from the back. The road was blocked. Richard was confused. He went back riding his donkey, bewildered.

One of the police officers who was conducting the race, stopped him. He said that Baudet had been adjudged the first. Tears of joy poured from Richard's eyes. "But how?" The first donkey was declared disqualified, he was told. When Richard showed the certificate and the prize to Mother, she was very happy. She gave a toffee to Richard for Baudet. Then she gave another to the rider.

"She must have realised that I would not give it to Baudet if one was given, Richard smiled. Perhaps Mother had a purpose in bringing the two kids together, thought he, retrospectively.

Notes and References

1. Sujata Nahar. *Mother's Chronicle*. Mysore; Mirra Aditi centre. Book-1. p.63.
2. *Mother's Chronicle*. Book-3. pp.131-33.
3. *Mother's Chronicle*-3. pp.136-37.
4. *Mother's Chronicle*-3. pp.137-38.
5. *Mother's Chronicle*-3. pp.139-40.
6. *The Mother. Collected Works*. Pondicherry; Sri Aurobindo Ashram. Centenary Edition. 1978. V-4. p.27.
7. *The Mother*. V-4. pp.27-28.
8. *The Mother*. V-4. pp. 322-23.
9. *The Mother*. V-9. p.100.

6

Mother's Flower Sense

Mother (The Divine Mother to her children) could enter the heart of a flower in a subtle way and identify herself with it. Through the flowers, she could convey to others her messages, thoughts and feelings. Through them she bestowed her blessings that were full of light, love and power.

Scientists asserted long ago that plants have life, feelings and memory. Distinguished astrophysicist, Dr. S. Chandrasekhar, through a series of lectures, tried to prove that it is the beauty of an object that motivates the scientists to discover the truth behind it. Mirra Alfassa had divine experiences from the age of five years. She received flashes of Truth in many mysterious ways. She too was moved by the beauty and harmony behind all creation. She wrote in her diary on 28 April 1917: "Lo! Here are flowers and benedictions! here is smile of divine love! It is without preferences and without repulsions. It streams out towards all in a generous flow and never takes back its marvellous gifts!"[1]

Roses blossom in response to their inner need of expressing beauty. The blossoming of flowers is an act of love. It is a great force of universal love and universal consciousness which makes all things blossom in beauty, she felt. She entered into the nature of the flowers, their inner truth by widening her consciousness in a mystic way. Thus she could know what they represented. To know the process of her identification with the plants and flowers, we have to look at her diary entry of 7 April 1917: "A deep concentration seized on me, and I perceived that I was identifying myself with a single cherry-blossom, then through it with all cherry-blossoms, and as I descended deeper in the consciousness, following a stream of bluish force, I became suddenly the cherry tree itself, stretching towards the sky like so many arms its innumerable branches laden with their sacrifice of flowers."[2]

Mirra Alfassa, painter, musician and occultist, came to meet Sri Aurobindo in India in quest of the Supreme Truth, and became his collaborator. The yogi recognized her as the Divine Mother. She managed the affairs of the Sri Aurobindo household giving formal birth to the Ashram at Pondicherry since 1926, after the master had gone into seclusion to bring down the Supramental Consciousness upon earth which was in existence at its primal shape, with the master and his few disciples. Since then she has been known as the Mother.

The Mother gave names to hundreds of flowers, according to their inner nature and spiritual significance, when they were brought to her by her ardent disciples from time to time. A book has been published listing more than 800 flowers named by her. The shape, size, colour and fragrance were the outer signs, apart from the inner significances of each flower that motivated her to name them.

Someone brought her tulsi *(Ocimum sanctum)*. She smelled it and said, "Oh 'Devotion'!" It is a fact that tulsi has been offered to Lord Krishna by the devotees from time immemorial. When datura (Angel's Trumpet) was brought likewise, she immediately named it 'Tapasya'. The flower is associated with Lord Shiva who is known for his ascetic practices or *tapasya.* The association of datura with Shiva is an age-old knowledge and tradition in India which the Mother could know through her intuitive perception, evoked by the vibration of the flower. The associations or connections of some such flowers with the respective Hindu Gods as we have referred are mere coincidences. It proves that the inner significances as Mother found were already reccgnised in Indian religious circle.

Holding a tiny yellow flower like a Dahlberg daisy *(Thymophylla tenuiloba)* between her fingers, she said, "I have always found that this one has a cleansing fragrance; when you breathe it, ah, everything becomes clean — it's wonderful!" She had her cold cured with the fragrance of this flower. She named it 'Mental Simplicity'.

Talking about the naming of flowers, the Mother once related an old Chaldean legend. A divine being was incarnated upon earth to awaken in it the supreme love. As usual, he was persecuted, tortured and wounded. He took refuge in an Arabian desert, under a small pomegranate tree. Nourished by the falling blood of the being on the soil, the tree grew to be enormously healthy and strong. Its bush was covered with marvellous scarlet flowers. She named the plant 'Divine's Love'. Iris is a noble flower, standing erect on its stalk. Its form has been stylised in the *fleur-de-lis,* emblem of the king of France. Mother named it 'Aristocracy of Beauty'. Mother named the hibiscus 'Power'. It is traditionally offered to Kali, the Goddess of Power, in India. Stories behind the naming of each flower by Mother, coinciding in many cases with the age-old practices and uses in India, which she had not known, must be interesting to all enthusiasts.

A flower is a manifestation of the psychic presence, Mother said. The whole life of a plant is dedicated to the worship of light. And their aspirations are intense. Look at a rose opening in the morning at the first touch of the sun, it's a magnificent self-giving in aspiration, she opined.

Flowers are very receptive. Those which she named could easily receive the force, the state of consciousness that she put into them, to transmit to others. Mother asked her children to be like a flower—a flower which is open, frank, generous and kind. She blessed those who came to her with flowers in answer to the aspirations coming from the depth of their being. Flowers were the medium. It all depended on the receptivity of the person receiving the flowers.

We have many photos of Mother giving her blessings with flowers. Even now her blessings are regularly sent to distant places in nice, small packets, consisting of petals of rose. And her ever-increasing number of devotees eagerly wait to receive them.

While explaining his integral yoga, Sri Aurobindo gave psychological analysis of different levels of human consciousness and parts of his being. Many flowers were named by Mother in relation to such planes and parts of our being.

Sri Aurobindo thus played an important part, though indirectly, in naming the flowers according to their spiritual significance. She spoke much more than she wrote. Whatever she said throughout her life, was for the progress of humanity: "What we want is that humanity should progress, whether it professes to lead a yogic life or not matters little, provided it makes the necessary effort for progress." She said on 25 December 1950.

Let us conclude with the words of Sri Aurobindo: "Flowers are moment's representations of things that are in themselves eternal."

Notes and References

1. *Prayers and Meditations. The Mother. Collected Works.* Centenary Edition. Pondicherry; Sri Aurobindo Ashram. V-1. p.362.
2. *Prayers and Meditations.* p.359.

Work Cited

Flowers and Their Messages. The Mother. Auroville; Auropress Trust. India. 1973.

7

An Artist Extra Mundane

Mirra Alfassa, later known as the Mother, could have been named as one of the greatest among the artists of her time, had she so desired. There is no doubt about that. But this was not to be so as she had no desire for fame. The truth of this statement will be obvious as we gradually unfold the tale of Mother's life as an artist and her attitude towards art.

In a world of uprising industrial bourgeoisie and burgeoning nouveau riche, an entirely commercial world, art had lost its dignity. It became "entirely commercial, obscure and ignorant from the beginning of the last century to its middle," Mother said in 1953.[1]" Such was the opinion of many other artists. Max Raphael said, "Using art to decorate private houses, to display the owner's wealth or so called culture is a barbarism."

Art in the field of advertisements is a controversial subject. The position continued up to 1875 after which there was a grand revival due to revolt by artists, writers and intellectuals. Mother later said that it was the era of impressionists, the era of Monet. She considered it to be a brilliant period. And it was during this period, at the end of the nineteenth century, that Mirra Alfassa stepped into the field of art. She began to draw from the age of eight, learned oil and other painting techniques when she was 10 and at the age of 12, she was already doing portraits.

Great artists, pioneers in art, were at work in Paris. Mirra, having completed her regular schooling at the age of 15, joined the Academie Julian as an art student, working eight hours a day. There she remained up to 1897. In 1892, when she was 14, one of her charcoal drawings, titled "Le Pont de la Divonn"

(Am) was put up at the international 'Blanc et Noir' exhibition in Paris. She had done it during a visit to her maternal grandmother, in a place near the Swiss border. At the age of 14 she started teaching painting to a small group of children. In spite of being the youngest she was respected for her personality and her ability to solve problems that baffled even those much senior to her throughout her stay at the Academie Julian. She received a thorough classical training there and was soon able to go beyond the formulae of the French academic style.

She was all praise for the beauty of the cathedrals in Venice where she went to a trip with her mother when she was 15 years old. On a subsequent visit, she made a painting of the Cathedral of St. Mark. On 13 October 1897 she married Henri Morisset who was her elder by eight years. In early 1898, the couple visited Pau, a town in the south west of France, to paint murals in a small church named after Saint James of Compostela in Spain, a close associate of Jesus Christ and who, it is said, appeared on a white horse, bathed in golden light, resembling the 'Kalki' of the Hindus. It was he who vanquished the Moors. Out of eight panels, Henri painted four. Mirra painted the lower part of one such panel called 'Apothesis', depicting the vanquished and slain Moors, as she could not climb the ladder to paint the upper portion. Both Mirra and Henri Morisset were hailed as true artists. Their works still remain there. She was in Normandy for some time where she did some paintings. 'Lady on a staircase' was one of them.

During the period of her life with Henri Morisset from 1897 to 1908 she was preoccupied with art despite her gradual absorption into her inner-self. Simultaneously, she was involved in occultism and painting. Most of her paintings belong to this period. Morisset was regularly exhibiting his paintings since 1898 at the 'Salon de la Sociét National des Beaux-Arts' in Paris. Mirra's works were also exhibited there titled, 'Salon', 'Dans Latelier' in 1903; 'Nature mort' and 'Vestibule' in 1904; 'La console', 'Bibelots' in 1905. Other titles have not been identified. Mirra and Henri were divorced in March 1908. This marked the end of a distinct phase of her life that was both artistic and vital. It brought her on a greater involvement in the occult region. None of the paintings done during the period from 1908 to 1915 could be dated definitely.

In early twentieth century, Mirra was introduced to systematic occultism through the great occultists Max and Alma Theon. She joined Theon's organisation in Paris and edited *Revue Cosmic*, the journal of the organisation. She had met Theon in Paris in 1905 and travelled to Algeria in 1906 and 1907. During that time, she made some paintings of the house and garden of Theon and also his portrait. Paul Richard, an intellectual giant, also visited Algeria in 1907 as he too was interested in occultism. He also joined their 'Le Cosmic' group in Paris. In association with Richard, Mirra gradually moved from the vital artistic world to the mental world, the world of intellect. They were married in 1911. Their mental development reached a high peak when she met Sri Aurobindo in 1914. After almost a year's stay in Pondicherry, both of them had to go back to Europe at the outbreak of the First World War, under political compulsion. After a short stay in Europe, they set out for Japan, where they reached on 18 May 1916.

The thirst for beauty and the impulse for its expression never left her. Mirra was overwhelmed seeing Japan for the first time. This is what she stated a couple of months later, on July 9, 1917: "The country is so wonderful, picturesque, many-sided, unexpected, charming, wild or sweet; it is in its appearance so much a synthesis of all the other countries of the world, from the tropical to the arctic, that no artistic eye can remain indifferent to it." Not only the beauty of the land but also the beauty of character of the Japanese people moved her. She found there the unity of art with life. "True art is a whole and an ensemble; it is one and of one piece with life. You see this intimate wholeness in ancient Greece and ancient Egypt . . . . It is like that in Japan or it was so till the other day before the invasion of a utilitarian and practical modernism," she said on 9 June 1954. She plunged into the Japanese lifestream in order to understand it better. And she learned the Japanese way of life—their language, culture, music, dress, water colour painting, and drawing. On 12 April

1951 she wrote, "I had everything to learn in Japan for four years, from an artistic point of view I lived from wonder to wonder." Some of her most beautiful works were done in Japan.

During the first year of their stay in Japan, Mirra and Paul lived in Tokyo, sharing a house with a young couple, Dr. S. Okhawa a professor and his wife. In 1918 Mirra spent the summer with Madam Okhawa in their house in Kyoto. It was here that she painted 'Lady on a verandah overlooking a lake.' In Kyoto. Mirra made another painting of her friend Nobuko Kobayshi, preparing medicine in her room. She also made a portrait of her in ink and a miniature portrait in oil on ivory which she presented to Kobayashi. When Rabindranath Tagore visited Japan and spoke at the Imperial University in Tokyo on 11 June 1916, Mirra made a pencil sketch of him on the same day. It was later rendered in ink, of which two versions are available. One of her outstanding portraits was of Hirasawa Tetsuo, a poet and an artist.

Richards visited the Daiunji temple in Sarashina, Nagano prefecture, about 200 km from Tokyo, between September 12 and 15, 1918. It is said that she was struck by its beauty and made a pencil sketch of this temple and its surroundings. She also made a couple of oil paintings and a long scroll on paper in Indian ink. This sketch was dated September 15, 1918 and was signed by her in Japanese. Before their departure Mirra made an ink sketch of Paul Richard in the temple 'visitor' book. It too was signed by her in Japanese. Paul Richard wrote a message in French. She passed from the vital-physical to a mental-intellectual field from 1908 up to 1914, which she defined as a mutual development where one has already understood that all ideas are true and that there is a synthesis to be made, and that there is something luminous and true beyond the synthesis.

She was essentially a spiritual being from her birth. She realised her mission on earth at the age of five. After seeing Sri Aurobindo, the Lord Krishna of her vision, in 1914 she truly surrendered herself to him and realised that her future work in the spiritual world was to be in collaboration with Sri Aurobindo in India. So to go back with Paul Richard under political compulsion, away from Sri Aurobindo, was an agonising experience for her. On board the ship Kamo Maru, on her way to Europe from Pondicherry, she wrote on 3 March 1915 in her 'Diary Notes' which was later published as "*Prayers and Meditations*: "Solitude, a harsh, intense solitude, and always this strong impression on having been flung headlong into a hell of darkness! Never at any moment of my life, in any circumstances, have I felt myself living in surroundings so entirely opposite to all that I am conscious of as true, so contrary to all that is the essence of my life... O Lord, what have I done that Thou hast thrown me thus into the sombre Night?"[2]

Though she reconciled with the situation later, became happier in Japan, the hiatus between the desired and apparent happiness remained unfulfilled. She was a worshipper of beauty. While in Japan this worship was tinged with spiritual love. She wrote in her Diary on 29 January 1917: "Beauty is the divine language in forms. And a consciousness of the Divine which is not translated externally by an understanding and expression of Beauty would be an incomplete consciousness....

"O Lord of Beauty . . . . Give me the perfect understanding of Thy Law so that I may not again fail to keep it. Love would be incomplete without Thee. Thou art one of its most perfect ornaments. Thou art one of its most harmonious smiles."[3] On 7 April 1917 she wrote, "O Japan, it is thy festive adorning, expression of thy goodwill, it is thy purest offering, the pledge of thy fidelity; it is thy way of saying that thou dost mirror the sky."[4]

Although she was enamoured of Japan and the Japanese during the period and lived from wonder to wonder, she learnt many new things, including the Japanese way of painting and produced many outstanding works, her inner life moved in much deeper waters and in higher spiritual ether. An idea of her feelings, realisations and conflicts of inner life is portrayed in the pages of her 'Diary Notes'. Not even for a moment did she forget her real work in India. In spite of the scenic beauty and other richness of Japan her spiritual thirst was not quenched. She felt something was missing there. In her talk of 12 April 1951 she spoke of Japan, "Not once do you have the feeling that you are in contact with something other than a marvellously organised mental-physical domain. Finally she returned to Pondicherry on 24 April 1920. On 22 June 1920 she wrote addressing God, "After granting me the joy which surpasses all expression, Thou hast sent me, O my beloved Lord, the struggle . . . out of struggle it is a more perfect realization of Thyself that must arise." She concluded as it was the most accomplished fact after her return finally to her desired place, near Sri Aurobindo in Pondicherry.[5]

To bring down the supramental light and force, supramental consciousness on earth was the mission of Sri Aurobindo through his newly-created path of Integral yoga. The Mother, after her second arrival, became his real soul-collaborator. After Lele, her received true help from her in his spiritual quest and achievements. He himself called her the 'Divine Mother'. She gradually took over the responsibility of maintaining Sri Aurobindo's household including himself and his disciples. After his Siddhi on November 24 1926 he withdrew into seclusion. Consequently, Mirra became the Mother and the guide of all inmates of Sri Aurobindo Ashram which actually took birth, as if by divine dispensation, on her assuming charge. She ran its affairs as a super-organiser till the last day of her mortal life on November 17, 1973. In Pondicherry she was deeply engaged in spiritual and organisational matters which took a great deal of her time and energy, not leaving much time for rest. Naturally she could no longer find the leisure to paint. However, her artistic impulse found spontaneous expression from time to time. Barring a few small oil paintings, she mostly did sketches and drawings in pencil, ink or charcoal.

One of the best oil paintings she did was titled 'Divine consciousness emerging from inconscient.' The story of this splendid work is different from the usual. Barindra Kumar Ghose, the younger brother of Sri Aurobindo, was practising oil painting under Mother's guidance in the early 1920s. As usual, at the end of each session he accumulated the unused paint in the palette on a small board. The board was gradually covered with a random mixture of colours. One day when he finished his work, Mother called for the palette and the board. At the centre of the board, in a few deft brush strokes, she completed the painting which was a face resembling Sri Aurobindo's, as if coming out of a chaos of colours resembling the inconscient. It is likely that Sri Aurobindo himself was present and Mother took the opportunity of making a quick portrait of him. She herself confirmed that it was the face of Sri Aurobindo. After this work there was a gap of 10 years. In 1931 she made Sri Aurobindo's portrait and a self-portrait in pencil. She also made many remarkable portraits of disciples in charcoal during this period. Some portraits were done between 1947 and 1949. Some were done in 1950. The last dated portrait was of Champaklal, her attendant disciple, on December 23 1959. Other than portraits, she made several animal studies—beautiful sketches of cats, a lion and a dog. She also made some drawings representing symbols and visions. Her drawing of a portrait of Champakial was done in February 1935 with her eyes closed. "The pencil just went on moving," she said to Sri Aurobindo.

Ascent to Truth is an extraordinary creation of a visionary dramatist. In her drama of the same title, the scene begins on a green plateau and a wide path which gradually narrows down leading towards a steep, rocky mountain which has seven levels. People from different stages of life with different vocations come together in search of Truth. It is a drama that reveals the Truth and aim of life of each seeker on their way to Truth. It shows how each fails until the last stage is reached when two aspirants take a leap from the summit with utmost faith, surrendering to the Divine. They reach their goal. A rock with a surrounding like in Mother's painting has been attempted on the seaside in Pondicherry. It deserves a look by the promenaders.

Mother helped and guided a number of her disciples in the Ashram to draw and paint. She encouraged and helped one of the disciples to illustrate Sri Aurobind's epic poem *Savitri*. She herself made some sketches for it as well. Connoisseurs thought highly of her work, many of which were gifted or sold during the earlier period of her painting career. Many of her works have decayed in the meantime due to wear and tear. It is said that only 40 of her paintings are now preserved along with some other kind of works. The time when Mother took to painting was a glorious period. French art and artistic works occupied a predominant position. During her time, the senior artists were Cezanne, Degas, Monet, Renoir and others.

Mother was a musician too and her circle of acquaintances was quite large. Some of her paintings were done in the studio of other artists like Abel Faivre and Charles Duvent and musicians like Erlanger. She had known Henry Morisset for quite a few years before their marriage. Among the list of artists she knew well, were such famous names like Gustav Moreau, Henri Matisse and Auguste Rodin. She lived among artists who were 10, 20 or more years older than her. "I mingled with all the great artists of the time, and I was like their kid sister," she said. She moved with Morisset to the countryside in their Richard-Brasier car or travelled by cycle in search of a source for painting. They had their own studio. "There was an intense vital development during this period of my life ... and it all centred on studies: study of sensation, study of observation, study of technique, comparative studies and so on; even the study of taste, of smell, of hearing, with an entire scale of observations. I mean, a kind of classification of experiences", Mother reminisced. Though she had every chance, she never took art as a career. She lived among the great artists but what did she notice in them? They truly had a sense of beauty, but morally some were very cruel. "When you saw the man at house, he had a pretty limited contact with the artist he was; and generally he turned into quite a vulgar man, quite ordinary," she observed. Often there was absence of a true love. She was disillusioned. Hence arose the need for parting from her husband, as it happened in her drama, *Towards the Future.*

Mother's artistic ability—refinement of style, clarity and depth of vision, mastery of technique—have been lauded by many critics and artists. A number of her works were selected for display at the National Salon and some of her paintings were sold too. But she did not pursue her career to establish herself as a great artist because, "I don't see any necessity of being the greatest artist, the greatest musician. That has always seemed to me a kind of vanity," she said on February 10 1954. One of her surviving remarks about the exhibition in the Salon was a sarcastic one about the President of the Republic, inspecting the pictures and passing childish remarks, for he was quite an ignoramus on the subject but the artists thronged round him and gave him great importance. "For such indeed is the vital in human beings—ravenously hungry for fame," she felt. She disliked such things from the beginning. Her greatest motive for painting, music, literature was the development of consciousness,; even of each part of the body like hands and eyes. She could paint without looking at the object. She could draw in seconds without break, a beautiful portrait. When she played the organ, beings from other worlds came and vied with each other for a minute's possession of her hand. Yogis are concerned with the highest aim of their life, a realisation of the divine consciousness. The best paintings and statues in India were done by Buddhist monks who preferred to remain unknown because "They do not consider their art-expression as the most important part of their life and do not put so much time and energy into it as mere artist," she said on May 30 1956. Though they are very few, Mother said, true artists are like yogis who create according to their inner vision. The physical world is the world of forms and perfection of form is beauty, Mother thought. And she found beauty as the expression of the eternal. She herself was one of the greatest of yogis the earth has ever seen. We may elaborate our ideas about the Mother through a few dialogues between herself and her disciple.

> Disciple: Surely such masterpieces deserve to be found and kept safely. You had taken so much pains over them.
>
> Mother: It does not matter.
>
> Disciple: But, Mother, don't you think there will be a loss if they are not preserved?
>
> The Mother with eyes far away yet full of tenderness for the agitated disciple said in a half-whisper: "You know, we live in eternity."[6]

However, Sri Aurobindo Ashram collected and reproduced in print her works, as much as possible, in 1992. This publication has been one of our main sources of information about Mother as an artist. The story of Mother's life as an artist can also he found in her collected works. Mother was a thousand-stringed instrument, that resounded with the profound music of her very being, enabling the spellbound audience of the world to a loving surrender at her feet.

Notes and References

1. Sujata Nahar. *Mother's Chronicle*, Book-Two Mysore; Mira Aditi Centre 1986. p. 19.
2. *Prayers and Meditations. The Mother. Collected Works of the Mother*, Centenary Edition. Pondicherry; Sri Aurobindo Ashram. 1979. V-1. p.291.
3. *Prayers and Meditations*. p.349.
4. *Prayers and Meditations*. p.359.
5. *Prayers and Meditations*. p.373.
6. K.D. Sethna. *The Mother: Past, Present and Future*. Jaipur; Kamal Gambhir. 1977. p. 9.

8

The Great Waves of Music

There is an unheard music in the heart of the deepest silence. Nature has a silent music. Man has been growing up with music from the beginning of time. The oldest musical instruments date back to 7000 B.C. For instance, flutes made of hollowed bones of red-crowned cranes, have been unearthed in China, as reported in *The Hindu* dated 25.9.1999.

"Who is there who in logical words can express the effect music has on us?" asked Carlyle. And he himself answered, "A kind of inarticulate unfathomable speech which leads us to the edge of the infinite and lets us for moments gaze into that." Plato in his *Republic* gave great importance to music in education. Through music one can understand the temperament of a people. "Change the musical system of a country, in course of time its constitution will be changed," said he. And Confucius said, "The music of a peaceful and prosperous country is quiet and joyous, and the government is orderly; the music of a country in turmoil shows dissatisfaction and anger, and the government is chaotic; and the music of a destroyed country shows sorrows and remembrance of the past, and the people are distressed. Thus we see that music and government are directly connected with one another."[1]

Aristotle in his *Poetics* expressed a similar thought in different words. He felt that the movements of music correspond to the moods of man's soul. And he added that music also has a cathartic effect on the listeners. Music is a great unifier. Through music, nations are able to bond together. It is reported that after playing the violin in the company of Pandit Ravishankar and Ali Akbar Khan at the St. Giles Cathedral at Edinburgh in 1965, the great maestro Yehudi

Menuhin drew the attention of the audience towards the fact that music had brought together on a common platform a Hindu, a Muslim and a Jew.

Though Laotse and Chuangtse, who belonged to one of the world's oldest civilisations, spoke little about music, Confucius spoke a good deal about it. He said that music rises from the heavens. Sages create music to correlate with heaven and create rituals to correlate with the earth. Music proceeds upon the principle of harmony in the universe. The harmony of spirit springs from the soul and blossoms forth in the form of music. Music rises from the human heart. When the emotions are touched, they are expressed through sounds. Man tries to create harmony in the human heart by a rediscovery of human nature and tries to promote music as a means towards the perfection of human culture. Music illustrates the primordial forces of nature.

Character is the background of human nature and music is the flowering of character. The song gives expression to our voice, Confucius said. In another place he has said that tones rise from the human heart and music is connected with the principle of human conduct. Therefore animals know the sounds but do not know the tones and common people know the tones but do not know the music. The universal impulse to enjoy the beauty and attractiveness of sounds, colours and forms, if denied proper training and self- purification, may lead one to go for the trivial, gaudy, sensuous, cheap and vulgar. So Sri Aurobindo recognised the immense educative value of music, painting and sculpture.

"Whenever a child comes to learn music, never refuse him. Every child has a right to learn music. Whether he becomes a musician or not is another matter but all must have the opportunity to learn music of some sort in order to appreciate it. You know, music is a great purifying force. In Europe every child learns music from their childhood . . . . So try to give them some music," Mother had said to the music teacher of the Sri Aurobindo Ashram School in 1965 during a conversation with her. Along with music and other studies, Mother gave a lot of importance to physical education. In this connection we again refer to the great teacher, Plato. He thought that music and gymnastics are the two essential items of education. But if it is based exclusively on music, it will produce softness and effeminacy in the character of the pupils, he thought. Only gymnastics will, on the other hand, produce hardness and brutality. So he professed a combination of both.

From ages past, the literati has spoken about music in various ways. Among them Shakespeare, as expected, spoke most dramatically about it:

"The man that hath not music in himself and is not moved with concord of sweet sounds, is fit for treason, stratagem, and spoils; let no man trust him."

As we come to the Mother, the mystery of music is unfolded before us through her vision on the subject. "Music is a means of expressing certain thoughts, feelings, emotions, aspirations. There is even a region where all these movements exist and from there, as they are brought down, they make a musical form. One who is a very good composer with some aspiration will produce very beautiful music for he is a good musician. A bad musician also may have a very high inspiration ... but as he possesses no musical capacity, what he produces is terribly commonplace, ordinary, uninteresting . . . . it is the origin of music, the inspiration from beyond, which is important; it is not purely the sounds, it is what the sounds express."[2]

In response to a question she said, "All physical life has the vital and mental life as its origin. The mental and vital realities have themselves another origin, and so on. Nothing can be manifested physically upon earth that has not a higher truth as its origin, otherwise the world would not exist."[3]

Asked, "From what plane does music generally come?" Mother replied: "There are different levels, There is a whole category of music that comes from the higher vital, which is very catching, somewhat (not to put it exactly) vulgar, it is something that twists your nerves . . . . There is one type of music which has vital origin . . . . And then there is music which has a spiritual origin, it is very bright and it carries you away, captures you entirely."[4]

But such things necessarily pass through the human vital before it is executed and without a vital strength and splendour the higher things are rendered vapid. The true value of creation depends on its source and on the vital capability of the composer. And as for the music of the concert and the cinema, she said there is an extraordinary skill in the making of such music, but it has an extraordinary vulgarity too. It seizes one in the solar plexus and it is this that one usually remembers. It is made vitally with vital vibrations, but what is behind is frightful.

About rock and pop music she felt that one in a thousand perhaps was good. "Should one waste one's time finding out one such music?" she asked during the same talks on 27 May 1953. Sri Aurobindo had said about the effect of popular music on the people:

"Rudyard Kipling's Barrack Room Ballads exercise a more universal appeal than was ever reached by Milton or Keats ... a band on the pier at a seaside resort will please more people than a great piece of music with the orchestration conducted by Sir Thomas Beecham . . . . It is usually the inferior things that have the more general if not quite universal appeal."[5]

The famous sitarist and great musician, Pandit Ravishankar had said during an interview given to *The Hindu* at his 78th year:

"The true soul of our music lies in its spiritual quality. And even in India this is getting bulldozed by the new trend of loudness. Performers and listeners want excitement all the time. With music we should close our eyes and feel some pain in the heart, feel like Praying and Meditating. Not jumping up to applaud."

In 1967 Mother said that the role of music lies in helping the consciousness to uplift itself towards the spiritual heights, repeating the similar words as she uttered years back in 1929, "Music too is an essentially spiritual art and has always been associated with religious feeling and an inner life."[6]

Between the year 1966 and 1968, once she said emphatically to the music teacher, **"Anything that lowers the** consciousness is no music for me and I don't want my children to listen to it."

Let us now hear from Mother about the world of creations, the source of all artistic inspirations, which she vividly described to her disciple on 27 October 1962. "I know it very well, I have been there frequently. It's at the very summit of human consciousness, on the borderline between what Sri Aurobindo calls the lower and the higher hemispheres. It is very high, very high. I have studied its realm extensively. It is a world of creation with several levels or degrees.

"The first zone you encounter is the zone of painting, sculpture, architecture: everything that has a material form. It is the zone of forms, coloured forms that are expressed as paintings, sculptures, and architecture. They are not forms as we know them, but rather typal forms; you can see garden types, for instance, wonderfully coloured and beautiful, or construction types.

"Then comes the musical zones, and there you find the origin of the sounds that have inspired the various composers. Great waves of music, without sound. It seems a bit strange, hut that's how it is.

"Beyond the musical zone lies thought: thoughts, organised thoughts for plays and books, abstractions for philosophies. But what used to interest me particularly were the combinations that gave birth to novels or plays.

"That is the third zone. What you find there are thought formations that are expressed in each person's brain in his own language. There are thought combinations for novels, plays, even philosophical systems. They are combinations of pure thought, not formulated in any language, but automatically expressed in each one's brain according to his particular language. It is the domain of pure thought . . . . These formations are at any one's disposal—nobody can say, 'It's my idea, it's My book.'

"Higher up, there is a fourth zone, a zone of coloured lights, plays of coloured lights. That's the order: first form, then sound, then ideas, then coloured lights.

"It's a zone of action, independent of form, sound and thought; it's above all that. A zone of active power and might you can use for a particular purpose—if you have the capacity to do so. That's the highest zone.

"When you go there and have the power, you can combine those forces so that they eventually materialize as creations on earth (it takes some time, it's rarely immediate).

"Each of these zones contain several levels, and the top of the musical zone is already starting to be ... waves of vibration. But it's still directly related to music, while those coloured forces I am speaking of have to do with terrestrial transformations and actions—great actions. They are powers of action. This zone where you hear no sound eventually is transformed to sounds and music. It is the summit. Each zone contains several levels. The waves of music are one particular mode of expression of those coloured waves—they should really be called 'luminous waves,' for they are self-luminous. Waves of coloured light. Great waves of coloured light.

"All those zones of artistic creation are very high up in the human consciousness, which is why art can be a wonderful tool for spiritual progress. For, this world of creation, is also the world of the gods; . . . ."[7]

The disciple was very interested to know the exact location of that musical zone. Mother replied:

"It's not exactly like geography, you know! But anyway, it's right on the border of the higher hemisphere. It's the first expression of Consciousness as joy. I remember finding the same vibration of joy in Beethoven and Bach (in Mozart also, but to a lesser degree). The first time I heard Beethoven's concerto in D—in D major, for violin and orchestra. . . suddenly the violin starts up (it's not right at the beginning—first there is an orchestral passage and then the violin takes it up) ... (Ysaye was playing, what a musician!), with the very first notes my head suddenly seemed to burst open, and I was cast into such splendour . . . . Oh, it was absolutely wonderful! For more than an hour I was in a state of bliss. Ysaye was a true musician!

". . . all my experiences came that way- unexpectedly, without my seeking anything . . . . One can get to that world directly from the vital, without going through all the mental gradations."[8]

Mother learnt music and painting as part of her routine education while studying other subjects. She did not put any special efforts to learn music, for she never had any idea of becoming one of the greatest musicians. In later years she came to be acquainted with many great musicians of her time, and she spoke about many masters and knew intimately about their creations. She played the organ as and when she felt like it. She played on Sundays and on some special occasions like the New Year. She was heard singing the year-end music in 1936 in her melodious voice with her own organ music. It charmed Abhoy Singh Nahar, then a teenager. The elan of her voice thrilled him.

How did she play the organ? She said on 20 October 1954:

"Before sitting down I don't even know what notes I am going to play. The region? It is always the same region ... it is a region very well known to me, one I frequent assiduously. But I do not at all know what will come. Nothing at all, nothing. I don't even decide what feeling or idea or state of consciousness is going to be expressed, nothing. I am like a blank page. I come and sit down, concentrate for a minute and let it come. Afterwards, sometimes I know, not always. But when I hear it a second time here, in the afternoon or evening, then I know; because it is no longer I, it is something that comes from outside."[9]

On 27 October 1962 she said, "I constantly hear something like great waves of music. I just have to withdraw a little, and there it is; I hear it. It is always there. It is music but without sound! Great waves of music. And whenever I hear those waves, my hands get the urge to play. So I am going to make some experiments: be completely passive, hands inert, and try to transcribe it . . . .

"I see it, you know, I see something like large orchestras around me, on my right, on my left—and I am supposed to transcribe it on a harmonium! It's like an orchestra made up of groups of musicians, with each group expressing one part of that combination, which is a much more complete sound than the ear can perceive . . . . It's not something you can express just by humming a little tune, but a whole body of musical vibrations. And as I hear it, I see how it should be expressed . . . . But it's another kind of vision; it's not the precise vision of the physical eye, but something very ... it's how consciousness sees, It's quite a total knowledge, which includes a vision, an awareness of the combination of sounds and how they should be expressed."[10]

About the regions harmonious and musical she said on 26 October 1955, "The sounds of material, physical music seem absolutely barbaric in comparison with that music! . . . All constructed instruments, among which the violin certainly has the purest sound, are very much inferior in their expression to the music of this world of harmonies."

About her hands remaining inert she said on 22 November 1967, "I knew how the consciousness works. Well, it is impossible to learn to play the piano or to paint unless the consciousness enters into the hands and the hands become conscious independently of the head. The head can be busy elsewhere, that has no importance."[11]

Sri Aurobindo also said that for any creation using hands, they should have their independent consciousness in them in order to create. Mother has suggested how we should listen to a piece of music in order to get the maximum benefit from it. First, we must have the sympathy and affinity for the piece of music that we are going to hear. The best way of listening is to be like a still mirror, totally very concentrated. By stopping to think, one may be able to make an inner opening. In a silent mind, the notes of music fall drop by drop whose sound alone remains. With the sounds, all the feelings, movements, emotions of the piece can be felt.

About her own music and its effect on the listeners she said that it depended on the inner condition of the listeners. At times they were well disposed towards it. Sometimes they were ill disposed, not able to understand what it conveyed. On 20 October 1968 Shobha Mitra, the music teacher, had asked

Mother about her plan of presenting Indian and Western music to the students and others for a proper understanding of classical music.

Mother said to her: "What is this, Indian music and Western music? Music is music. When it is manifested in the world atmosphere it is received by the musicians according to their receptivities, their surrounding, their cultural background . . . . It is the receptivity of the musician which differs in different parts of the world. But it is one music, one vibration, one purifying force coming straight from the supreme."

But Mother herself had expressed her well considered opinions about the two types of music and musicians of the two systems at other times.

In reply to a question about the differences between the two types of music, on 27 May 1953 she said, "Very high inspiration comes only rarely in European music; rare also is the psychic origin, very rare. The expression is almost always, except in a few rare cases, a vital expression—interesting, powerful. Most often, the origin is purely, vital. Sometimes it comes from the very heights, then it is wonderful. Sometimes it is psychic, particularly in what has been religious music, but this is not very frequent.

"Indian music... has almost always a psychic origin; for example, the ragas have a psychic origin . . . . The inspiration often does not come from above. But Indian music is very rarely embodied in a strong vital. It has rather an inner and intimate origin. I have heard a great deal of Indian music, a great deal; I have rarely heard Indian music having vital strength, very rarely . . . . perhaps not more than four or five times . . . . it is very tenuous, very subtle, as there are none of those intense vital vibrations, one can easily glide within it and climb back to the psychic origin of the music. It has that effect upon you. It is a kind of ecstatic trance, as from an intoxication . . . . the music is so tenuous that there is no response from the vital, it leaves you altogether flat. Sometimes, there was a vital force, then it became quite good . . . . I myself like this music very much, this kind of theme developing into a play . . . variations, innumerable variations, and it is always the same theme which is developed in one way or another. In Europe there were ... true musicians and they too had the thing. Bach had it . . . Mozart had it . . . it was music for music's sake . . . . personally I find it wonderful to put you in repose, and you enter deep within yourself . . . it gives you the psychic consciousness: something that makes you withdraw from the external consciousness, which makes you enter elsewhere, enter within."[12]

Mother highly praised the songs of Mirabai, music of Thyagaraja and the Rishis of yore. Some are of the opinion that in modern India all other things have been influenced and mixed with borrowd ideas from the other countries. Only Indian classical music remains pure and unmixed. It has a steady, ever increasing demand to the real lovers of music. Mother discussed about a few maestros of Western music from time to time. We may quote a few examples for understanding her musical preferences:

I consider that man (Berlioz) one of the purest expressions of music. I could say that he is an incarnation of music, of the spirit of music. Unfortunately his body was very frail, ... there was no physical pain which was not instantaneously translated into music in him; that is, the spirit of music was much stronger than human pain, and each blow which he received from life was translated into music. It is something very rare. . . . His power of orchestration was very, very remarkable. When one can orchestrate something for six hundred performers, it means a science as complicated as the most complicated mathematics. And in fact they come very close," she said on 20 October 1954.[13]

"Cesar Frank played on the organ as one inspired; he had an opening into the psychic life and he was conscious of it. Beethoven, when he composed the ninth symphony, had the vision of an opening into a higher world and of the descent of a higher world into this earthly plane. Wagner had strong and powerful intimations of the occult world; he had the ... sense of the occult and through it he received his greatest inspiration. Some of the glimpses he had were of an exceptional beauty, as in Parsifal, in some parts of Tristan and Iseult and mostly in its last great act," she replied on 28 July 1929.[14]

Speaking about the world of harmony she gave an example of how two great artists had drawn inspiration from that source. For instance, "there is a certain line of music, consisting of a few supreme notes, that was behind the production of two artists who came one after another—one a concerto of Bach, another a concerto of Beethoven. The two are not alike on paper and differ to the outward ear, but in their essence they are the same."[15]

About the concerto of Bach, Mother said, he received less but it was the purer of the two. In describing his work, Mother said, "The vibration was that of the victorious emergence of consciousness, consciousness tearing itself out of the womb of unconsciousness in a triumphant uprising and birth."[16]

Sri Aurobindo Ashram has recorded some 39 pieces of her organ music of different durations—from eight to 30 minutes. These are maintained and are re-recorded as and when needed. They are played with other pieces of her readings and talks. Some of her music was recorded. Some might have remained unrecorded, for each time she was not ready for recording them.

She reminisced, once when she was in Algeria, a big frog used to come and listen to her music silently. And it was distinctly disapproving, when she stopped playing! She did not teach her music in the usual way. Little was to be taught, for it had an occult origin. "It cannot be copied," she said to the music teacher. But some of her disciples who had some inclination to learn her kind of music and bad the capacity, learnt it to the extent possible. She not only played the organ, she was also a great music composer. She was a teacher's teacher with her subtle understanding and capacity for the occult understanding and penetration into the subject through it. Her music is for meditation. She herself was music.

At the end of the year 1964 she was aged almost 87 years. She realised the state of her failing health. And she had many involvements. Though she wanted to allow her hands to play, for practical reasons she could not so do. "But for that, I would need some time ... not to be caught in the cogwheels of a regulated life, she said on 28 November 1964."[17] Her surrounding atmosphere was not favourable either.

Hearing the beautiful music of Sunil Bhattacharya, one of her disciples, she took a decision on 28 November 1964, not to play the music for the next New Year. She decided to give up music. And she entrusted the job to Sunil.

"I have decided not to play this year for January 1st. Even last year I very much hesitated to play because I was absolutely conscious of the inadequacy- the poorness and inadequacy- of the physical instrument ... it wasn't worth much."[18]

Notes and References

1. *The Wisdom of Confucius*. Lin Yutang. New York: The Modern Library. 1938. p. 252.
2. *The Mother. Collected Works*. Centenary Edition. 1978. Pondicherry; Sri Aurobindo Ashram. V-5. pp. 69-70.
3. *The Mother*. pp. 70-71.
4. *The Mother*. p.75.
5. Sri Aurobindo. *The Future Poetry*. Pondicherry; Sri Aurobindo Ashram- S.A.B.C.L. 1972. V-9. p. 482.
6. *The Mother*. op. cit. V-5. p. 76.
7. Satprem. *Mother's Agenda*. Paris; Institut De Recherches Evolutive. 1962. Translated in 1982. V-3. pp. 387-390.
8. *Mother's Agenda*. p. 391.
9. *The Mother*. V-6. p. 384.
10. *Mother's Agenda*. op. cit. P. 387-388.
11. *The Mother*. V-7. p. 351.
12. *The Mother*. V-5. pp. 77-78.
13. *The Mother*. V-6. pp. 379-80.
14. *The Mother*. V-3. p.111.
15. *The Mother*. V-3. p.112.
16. *The Mother*. V-3. p.113.
17. *Mother's Agenda*. op. cit. V-5. p. 298.
18. *Ibid*. V-5. p. 297.

9

Mother's Literature

"I am no poet," Mother had once said. But she was indeed a poet, as we see through some of her prose works. She wrote plays that were performed by the students of the school. All her plays are serious, idealistic and educative. Though she never claimed to be a poet or a littérateur, her works give ample proof of her literary talent. She had a very clear idea and view about what literature is.

"One must have the taste for forms, for a beautiful way of saying things, a little exceptional, not too banal; but it is just one way, it's a way of saying things which is charming. Literature exists completely in the way of saying things. You catch what you can of what's behind. If you are indeed open to the literary meaning, it evokes things for you; but it cannot be explained. It is a means of evocation which corresponds also with music. Naturally, one can analyse literature and see how the sentence is constructed, but this is like your changing a human being into a skeleton. It is not pretty, a skeleton, "she said, in answer to a question on 21 September 1955."[1]

She always praised the beauty of form, expression, contents and ideas in literature. She was very aware of all popular but vulgar creations, and always asked her followers to desist from entering such houses or devouring such work. During the same question and answer session she said, "All this happens because from the point of view of production they succeed in making things very cheap, what are called popular "accessible to all . . . the more it sells the better it is. It may be frightful, but it's very good if it sells well. It's the same thing with art, the same thing with the drama . . . .

"And the whole world is drowned under these things, to such an extent that when there's someone who has written a good book or a fine play, there is no longer any place for him anywhere, because the whole place has been taken up by these things."[2]

Her own style was direct, penetrating and poetic. A few examples will illustrate the point. "Each time that a heart leaps at the touch of Thy divine breath, a little more beauty seems to be born upon the Earth, the air is embalmed with a sweet perfume, all becomes more friendly. . . .

"At the blessed hours all earth sings a hymn of gladness, the grasses shudder with pleasure, the air is vibrant with light, the trees lift towards heaven their most ardent prayer, the chant of the birds becomes a canticle, the waves of the sea billow with love, the smile of children tells of the infinite and the souls of men appear in their eyes. . . .

"Drop by drop Thou allowest to fall in a fertilising rain the living and redeeming flame of Thy Almighty love. . . . one would say a rain upon earth of golden stars one by one from a sombre firmament."[3]

Again, "You who weep, who suffer and tremble, who dare not expect an end to your ills, an issue to your pangs, behold: there is no night without dawn and the day is about to break when darkness is thickest; there is no mist that the sun does not dispel, no cloud that it does not gild, no tear that it will not dry one day, no storm that is not followed by its shining triumphant bow; there is no snow that it does not melt, nor winter that it does not change into radiant spring. . . .

"Every grain that is sown in the earth produces a thousand. Every wing-beat of sorrow can be a soaring towards glory. . . .

"That is how, in this despised and desolate but fruitful and blessed Matter, each atom contains a divine thought, each being carries within him the Divine inhabitant. And if no being in all the universe is as frail as man, neither is any as divine as he!

"In truth, in truth, in humiliation lies and cradle of glory!"[4]

Apart from short stories and plays, Mother wrote many articles which were published between 1949 and 1955 in the *Bulletin of the Ashram Centre of Education.* All of them are educative, original, written with a force.

Sri Aurobindo divided a human being into four main planes: psychic, mental, vital and physical. All of them contribute towards the making of a man. A harmonious development of all the four parts makes a man great. Mother based her education on the development of the four main human faculties. 'The Science of Living' and 'The Four Austerities and the Four Liberations' are the most illuminating of all the articles in this group. They are about the four parts of the human being. Mother also wrote separately on Physical, Mental, Vital, Psychic and Spiritual education. She began her 'The Science of Living' with a sub-heading "To know oneself and to control oneself." The first sentence of the first chapter is: "An aimless life is always a miserable life."

In both the articles she stressed on the observation of certain disciplines, austerities and restraints with utmost sincerity so that they become a kind of '*tapasya*' but without inflicting any injury to one's being. The four austerities will lead to four liberations, she said. The psychic and emotional liberation—liberation of the feeling—will be at the same time the liberation from suffering. The mental liberation or liberation from ignorance will establish in the being the mind of light or the gnostic consciousness. It will give creative peace and serenity and the power which results from them. Physical liberation is the liberation from the material cause an effect.

In 'The Science of Living' she said, "The psychic will be the vehicle of true and pure love, the mind will be the vehicle of infallible knowledge the vital will manifest an invincible power and strength and the body will be the expression of a perfect beauty and harmony."[5]

Among her other articles, 'Transformation,' 'The Fear of Death', 'Four methods of conquering it', 'Helping Humanity' and others are unique in their own way. She wrote some short articles at the beginning of the twentieth century. Among such articles, written in 1910 and onward, 'On Thought', 'On

Dreams', 'The Supreme Discovery' are remarkable not only for the valuable teaching but also for their literary expression.

In answer to a question, "Which minds are nearest to me and what is my ideal work among them?"—Mother wrote an essay which was read to a group of seekers on 2 July 1912. A few excerpts from the essay will prove how deep and far reaching were her observations and how deftly they were expressed. It is not just a pure heart but also luminous thoughts and lofty ideals that help create great literature.

"Always, in one way or another, life puts in our path those who for some reason are near to us. Each individual creates his own environment according to what he is himself . . . .

"If we observe attentively the causes which bring us closer to our kind, we see that these contacts occur at various levels of depth in our being, depending on our own special mode of conscious activity.

"We can classify these relationships into four main categories corresponding to our four principal modes of activity: physical, vital, psychic and mental . . . .

"Physical contact is compulsory, so to say, since it depends on the fact that we have a physical body. . . .

"With certain exceptions, material help is the best assistance we can give to the members of our family or to those whom we chance to meet in the street, in trains, in ships, in buses, etc. : pecuniary help, aid in case of illness or danger.

"We should never forget that the duration of a contact between two human lives depends on the number and depths of the states of being in which the affinities that bind them have their play. . . .

"Only those are friends forever who have been close or distant friends for all time in this or other worlds . . . .

"When we become one with the inner Godhead, we become one in depth with all, and it is through Her and by Her that we must come into contact with all beings. Then, free from all attraction and repulsion, all likes and dislikes, we are close to what is close to Her and far from what is far from Her."[6]

She wrote some articles during her days in Japan between 1916 and 1920. Among them 'Impressions of Japan', 'The Children of Japan' 'To the Women of Japan' are thought-provoking and beautiful.

On the occasion of the Supramental Manifestation (a higher spiritual light and force) on earth on February 29 1956, she described the event in her usual symbolic expression:

"This evening the Divine Presence, concrete and material, was there present amongst you. I had a form of living gold, bigger than the universe, and I was facing a huge and massive golden door which separated the world from the Divine.

"As I looked at the door, I knew and willed, in a single movement of consciousness, that 'the time has come,' and lifting with both hands a mighty golden hammer I struck one blow, one single blow on the door and the door was shattered to pieces.

"Then the Supramental Light and Force and Consciousness rushed down upon earth in an uninterrupted flow."[7]

Besides what she wrote to teach, to give advices or to guide, to tell her experiences and just to tell stories from life and mythology, she talked mostly in collective classes and meetings. But in answer to her disciples and various other persons she talked person to person too. Her question and answers comprise the greater volume of her works full of meaning with beauty of expression, emotion of sincere goodwill for all her children. Such talks and answers are part of her literature.

Notes and References

1. *The Mother. Collected Works*. Centenary Edition. Pondicherry; Sri Aurobindo Ashram. 1979. V-7. p.308.
2. *The Mother*. V-7. pp. 310-11.
3. *Prayers and Meditations. The Mother*. V-1. pp.356-57.
4. *The Supreme Discovery. The Mother*. V-2. pp. 42-44.
5. *The Mother*. op. cit. V-12. p.8.
6. *Ibid*. V-2. pp. 68-70.
7. *Ibid*. V-13. p.52.

Dramas

10

Towards the Future

During the first quarter of the twentieth century, while talking to women in Japan, Mother remarked about the position of women in the society in the following words:

"It is true that, as soon as great events and works are in question, the custom is to relegate women to a corner with a smile of patronising contempt which means: this is not your business, poor, feeble, futile creatures . . . . And women, submissive, childlike, lazy perhaps, have accepted, at least in many countries, this deplorable state of things. I dare to say that they are wrong. In the life of the future, there shall be no more room for such division, such disequilibrium between the masculine and the feminine. The true relation of the two sexes is an equal footing of mutual help and close collaboration."[1]

Let us now quote from a very famous play with which, it may be said, the concept of modernism in modern drama started.

Helmar — "Try to come down now, and get back to normal, my poor frightened little song-bird. Don't you worry—you will be safe under my wings—they'll protect you. . . . Nora! You'll be sheltered here, I'll cherish you as if you were a little dove I'd rescued from the claws of some dreadful hawk. You'll see — your poor fluttering little heart will soon grow calm again."

Already a complicated issue has come up between them. The very idea about a wife (here Nora) of her husband Helmar is the cause of a tumultuous revolt, more in the inner world of the little song-bird than outside. So says Nora, after some more talk:

> "It doesn't occur to you, does it, that though we've been married for eight years, this is the first time that we two - man and wife - have sat down for a serious talk?
>
> Helmar: "But, Nora, darling - why should you be concerned with serious thoughts?
>
> Nora: While I was still at home I used to hear Father airing his opinions and they became my opinions . . . He used to call me his doll-baby, and played with me as I played with my dolls. From Father's hands 1 passed into yours. You arranged everything according to your tastes, and 1 acquired the same tastes, or I pretended to. . . . I have lived here like a beggar, from hand to mouth.

When Helmar asks in astonishment after the unexpected outburst, whether she is happy with him, she replies, "No; only merry. You've always been so kind to me. But our home has never been anything but a play-room. I've been your doll-wife, just as at home I was papa's doll-child. And the children in turn, have been my dolls.

Finally Nora declares that she would leave him. Then Helmar at one point remarks:

> Helmar: You don't love me any more.
>
> Nora: No; that is just it.
>
> Helmar: And can you tell me when I lost your love?
>
> Nora: Yes, I can tell you. It was tonight . . . . I knew then you weren't the man I always thought you were.
>
> During the conversation she states again: At that moment it suddenly dawned on me that I had been living here for eight years with a stranger and that I'd borne him three children. I can't bear to think about it! I could tear myself to pieces!

After this, it is no longer possible for her to spend the night in a strange man's house. So she leaves him for ever, leaving behind her children, without any after thought, at midnight, slamming the door behind her. And the famous critic Huneker said, "That slammed door reverberated across the roof of the world."[2]

Indeed, it was an astonishing and significant revolt by a housewife against patriarchal society, in a play written as early as in 1879. And the play is Henrick Ibsen's *Doll's House.* The Mother comments elsewhere:

"In any case, the indisputable fact remains: man feels superior and wants to dominate, woman feels oppressed and revolts, openly or secretly; and the eternal quarrel between the sexes is perpetuated from age to age, identical in essence, innumerable in its forms and hues."[3]

So problem-stricken Stridenberg could not find a solution to this eternal problem. To him the essence of man's tragic dilemma is that there is no rational but only an irrational solution for this dichotomy of life. His was a reaction to Ibsenism. While Ibsen with his positive attitude separated the husband and wife in order to establish the rights of women, Stridenberg found that impossible. To him, even the hint of a solution, even through negation, was not acceptable. Hence in his *Sir Bingt's Wife,* while the husband and wife quarrel for the same reason as in *Doll's House,* they don't move apart. They are reconciled, not on any moral or rational basis hut because the husband says: "You did not want to love me because your pride forbade; but you love me anyway . . . . I wanted to hate you, I wished to kill you but still I love you."[4]

Joseph Woodcrutch in his foreword to *Modernism in Modern Drama* has drawn a very significant conclusion about modern literature, "The thesis I have tried to develop is that the modern drama of Europe and America, like modern literature in general, affords much material from the examination of which may be obtained a clear idea of what some of the radically new, or at least supposedly new, ideas were." The conclusion drawn is that at least certain of these ideas are such that they inevitably lead, not to a bright future, but to something like intellectual and moral paralysis.

It is evident that the reconciliation ultimately reached between husband and wife in *Sir Bingt's Wife* is more ominous than the parting of Nora. And the later dramas of the modern period depict such irreconcilable complexities of life in the plays of Pirandello, Eugene O'Neill, *Sean O'Casey* and many others.

The position and problems related to women have attracted the attention of many great men, from Aristotle to the current writers. But none, up to Ibsen's time, had presented the problem as did the latter. "To him marriage was so sacred that he believed it must be based upon a spiritual communion; mere 'living together' was not enough. He felt that a man and a woman should, ideally, go through life together as perfect equals, in perfect honesty, free to develop — each in his own way — into a complete human entity."[5]

Mother asserted that to be one in aspiration and ascension and to move forward at the same pace on the same spiritual path lies the secret of a lasting union between a married couple. By making Nora leave her husband forever Ibsen brought home his cherished idea that had Nora been respectfully and equally treated as an individual, she would not have left her home. He was different from many others in his view of the individual. He bade every individual reform himself before he proceeded to reform the society. Here again we may refer the Mother who said that the world will be made better only in proportion as we make ourselves better. She felt that the Vedantic truth stating that the world is only a projection, a function of our consciousness is as practical as spiritually true. She believed that the root of all evil lies in our ignorant nature. Ibsen also believed that all evils grow in the darkness. So O'svald Alving, the hero, while dying in his insanity calls out, "The Sun, Mother, give me the Sun" *(Ghosts)*. So this was Ibsen, the positivist, reformer, poet and pioneer of modernism in modern drama.

But if Ibsen was a revolutionary dramatist and if the sound of the slamming the door reverberated across the roof of the world, it was up to that, that's where it ended. Ibsen the poet and dramatist, though indirectly hinted at his positive aim, was not a social reformer and was content to show the problem. He was not interested in the solution in a direct way. But Mother, being the Divine Mother, was concerned with the well-being of the whole of humanity, to provide solutions to all problems and to give a proper direction to the lives of her children. Though she realised the problem of the sexes, it was not enigmatic to her. She saw the reason:

"Thus woman is enslaved to man because of the attraction she feels for the male and his strength, because of the desire for a home and the security it brings, and lastly because of the attachment to motherhood. Man too on his side is enslaved to woman, because of his possessiveness, his thirst for power and domination, because of his desire for sexual relations and because of his attachment to the little comforts and conveniences of married life.

"That is why no law can liberate women unless they liberate themselves; likewise, men too, in spite of all their habits of domination, will cease to be enslaved only when they have freed themselves from all inner enslavement."[6]

So in *Towards the Future,* the Mother advised the newly engaged couple:

"Do not allow your union to serve as an excuse for the satisfaction of animal appetites or sensual desires. On the contrary, make it a means of mutual help between you so that you may surmount yourselves in a constant aspiration and effort for progress towards perfect living."

If Doll's House was a revolutionary drama which shocked and stunned the conservatives, *Towards the Future* was greater in its silent revolution and its far reaching effects. If the problem of *Doll's House* was moral and social, *Towards the Future* leads us to a spiritual solution. "Blessed are those who take a leap towards the future," The Mother gave a message in 1971 and she was ever a futurist as was Sri Aurobindo.

Husband and wife, as in *Doll's House,* symbolise the common couple, found universally. The husband, an educated bourgeois is proud of himself. So full of self-esteem that he is ready to do everything for his wife but not give her the honour she deserves not even for love's sake. The wife is a beautiful doll; soft but pitiable. And when she realises her situation, her realisation brings about the clash between them. But in *Towards the Future* the couple is already on a high intellectual and social level. The husband is a poet and very influential in society. The wife is equally cultured with almost unrealisable dreams to reform mankind, to help humanity and to progress spiritually.

"My husband and I are very good friends, although that does not prevent us both from feeling very isolated. Esteem and mutual concessions create a harmony that makes life more than merely bearable. But is that happiness?"

The poet soliloquises about his wife:

> "Always the same kind of affectionate attentions. She never fails in her care and her sweetness. When look at her, it is like seeing light; her intelligence and kindness shine so brightly around her.... But all that is not love.... Love! What a dream!"
>
> (*Towards the Future*)

They possess all other essentials of life to be happy. No want. Why then the isolation? Why not happiness? Isolation lies at the deeper end of the heart. The realisation of the true love that is at the origin of the worlds, remains a dream to them. In ordinary lives thousands of people live like what they perhaps do not know; they do really have neither time nor the initiative to find out what kind of life they lead. To them it is a mechanical, morning-to-night carry-on process. But here the people are extremely sensitive, idealists, dreamers. So she says:

"There are unions without love, based on esteem and mutual concession which can be quite tolerable, but I consider that when love comes, everything else should give way to it."

Towards the Future is a *One Act* play where the story takes a definitive turn leading to the most desired aim. Here she shows us the possibility of a very pure and sincere solution to a complex problem; again, almost an unrealisable dream. The play begins with conversation between a school friend and the heroine, She. The school friend meeting her after a long absence is quite astonished to find that She, who all along was against marriage (for that was contrary to her ideals and nature) is married. In reply to the astonished queries of the friend she replies, "But you must do me the justice to admit that I never said anything against true love, the love that comes from a deep affinity and carries with it an identity of views and aspirations. I always dreamt of a great love shared, free from all animal activity; something that can translate physically the great love that is at the origin of the world."

She fails in her aspirations. But they continue peacefully with mutual esteem. In the meantime, a girl who happens to be a clairvoyant, the Musician, comes to stay near the Poet's house. She is a great musician and tries to get acquainted with people in her profession, to become one of them. But she knows no one. The Poet is charmed after only hearing her voice. While She goes out to her friend, a painter comes and offers to introduce him to the Musician who, it is said, already has great appreciation for the Poet's creations and seeks the help of the influential man, for which the poet is only too willing. The Painter introduces them and takes leave. The Poet and Musician feel drawn to each other and the Musician feels so relaxed that she sleeps on the cushions and the Poet strokes her forehead. Both feel an unprecedented happiness, peace and fulfilment. It seems (as if it was the moment they had both been waiting for throughout their lives) to be much more than mere love at first sight. It seems as if their union was preordained by some unknown, omniscient benefactor. But the Poet baulks at the idea of their being married, which the girl does not understand. Although the Poet is a comrade to She, the husband and wife have no love in the true sense. They only have respect for each other. But the bond cannot be broken so easily. The Poet is in a great dilemma. Meanwhile She comes back from her friend's house and quite dramatically appears on the scene—she declares that she has overheard the last tender and affectionate exchange between the two and then she tells them that they are free to lead their lives together, deciding to follow her noble aim of helping humanity, to reach a higher state of consciousness, and in that She hopes to get the help of those who hold the eternal wisdom and who have from a distance, guided our steps till now.

The Poet and the Musician are deeply moved. The Poet is full of sympathy and says: "I know you live always on the summit of your consciousness in a pure and serene light. But solitude is hard at times and the hour can be dull and sad." "She argues in a calm voice": Love is the only bond of legitimate union. The absence of love is enough to invalidate any union. Then she hastens to add, "My friend, you remember our pact. We promised each other full freedom the moment love would awaken in either of us."

Here we have a small question: did She marry the Poet knowing beforehand that there would be no love between them? We feel She married in order to realise true love which is the only basis of true union as She confessed to her friend and in the course of time her aspiration failed. For hope must have been the motive of her actions. This is of course our logic. However, She finally consoles the new couple saying:

"Now I know *for* certain that only one love can satisfy my living: it is the love for the Divine; it is the Divine love, for that alone never fails you. Perhaps one day I shall find the favourable conditions and the necessary help for the achievement of the supreme realisation, the transformation, the divinisation of physical being which will change the world into a blessed land all made of harmony and light, peace and beauty."

We remember the identical reply that Mother gave to one of her young disciple's question as to what is the real happiness and when does it come? "When one no longer feels any attraction for the other, false happiness. Real happiness is of Divine origin; it is pure and unconditioned."[7]

Prema Nandakurnar wrote about She: "She is altogether too pure and perfect, and belongs to regions above the aesthetic, being in fact a Savitri-like figure as portrayed in Sri Aurobindo's epic."[8]

She was perhaps too extraordinary, spiritual and beyond the sphere of ordinary human understanding. So there could not be any love between the Poet and She. The Musician is helpful and inspiring to the Poet—an ideal situation—as explained by the Mother elsewhere in a Women's Association:

"Since we want to learn to think better in order to live better, since we want to know how to think in order to recover our place and status in life as feminine counterpart and to become in effect, as we are in a latent way, the helpful, inspiring and equilibrating element, it seems to me indispensable that we should, first of all study what thought is."[9]

The heroine, She, accepted the only course left for such a personality whereas the opportunity given to the Poet and the Musician was the ideal for any ordinary, even higher intellectual level of humanity. She gave them the chance. And all of them took "A leap towards the future. "The solution is really ideal, beautiful and harmonious, almost without any grudge on any side." This is where it differs from Henrik Ibsen, Stridenberg and others.

Notes and References

1. *To the Women of Japan. The Mother. Collected Works*, Centenary edition. Pondichcriy; Shri Aurobindo Ashram. 1978. Vol -2. p. 155.
2. As quoted by Eva Le Gallienne in *Six Plays of Henrick Ibsen.* Introduction.
3. *The Problem of Women. The Mother. Collected Works*, op. cit. Vol-12. p. 103.
4. Joseph Wood Krutch. *Modernism in Modern Drama.* New York; Cornell University Press. 1966. Foreword.
5. Eva Le Gallienne. *Six Plays of Henrick Ibsen.* Introduction.
6. Mother. *The Problem of Women.* pp. 103-104.
7. *Bulletine of JAICE.* Issue-August, 1982. Pondicherry. p. 42.
8. Prema Nanda Kumar. *The Plays of the Mother.* Pondicherry; Sri Aurobindo Circle. 1978. p. 99.
9. *On Thought. The Mother. Collected Works*; op. cit. 1978. Vol - 2. p. 21.

Work Cited

On Education. Part-3; Dramas. The Mother. Collected Works. Centenary Edition. op. cit. pp. 455-472.

11

The Ascent to Truth

After *Towards the Future* Mother wrote two other plays—*The Great Secret* and *The Ascent to Truth.* While *Towards the Future* was produced on stage in 1949, *The Great Secret* was staged in 1954 and *The Ascent to Truth* in 1957. Unlike her other two plays, in *Towards the Future,* the pace of action is very fast, more mental and psychic than physical. There is suspense, there is a proper movement from beginning towards the desired end. Because of that many of us feel that this is the best of her plays and one of the best among her literary creations. There is an element of autobiography in it.

The Ascent to Truth in its dramatic form is identical with her painting of the *Hall of Aspiration.* There are some six turning points in *Towards the Future* and in *The Ascent to Truth;* there are seven stages with prologue and epilogue at the beginning and at the end. There is a sub-title to the play, 'A Drama of Life'. If one-act plays have resemblance to short stories, *The Ascent to Truth* is a beautiful, compact short story, unfolding through different stages the drama of life, both inwardly and outwardly. The symbol is very clear and transparent to one acquainted with the Yoga of Sri Aurbobindo. On the green valley stands a mountain towering towards the sky; climbing the mountain is the Ascent to Truth as accepted by a group of people representing a cross section of humanity, in a meeting held between them.

Here too there is no mention of the name of characters or places or period of action, thus indicating infinity in terms of time and space. The characters are The Philanthropist, The Pessimist, The Scientist, The Artist, The Students, Two Lovers, The Ascetic and Two Aspirants. All of them, in their own way have agreed to venture out to discover the truth, to complete their mission. With their varied experiences and expectations from life they have come to a common agreement that: "By uniting our efforts, we shall climb this sacred mountain that leads to the Truth. It is a difficult and arduous enterprise, but well worth the attempt, for when one reaches the summit, one can look upon the Truth and all problems must necessarily be solved." Each one of them aspires to realise the truth according to his own level of consciousness which is in accord with the part each have to play in life. All of them begin the journey with equal enthusiasm and energy and as they climb, each one's attitude changes according to respective capacities to soar higher.

Of course each one of them has his own justification and logic which is, as Sri Aurobindo puts it: "Logic claims and even honestly attempts to get rid of predilection and to see things in the same light of truth but it is not equal to its task; our nature is full of subtle disguises and, the moment we form an opinion, attaches itself to it and secretly takes it under its protection under pretence of an exclusive attachment to truth ... we perform the comedy with perfect sincerity, but it is still a comedy which nature plays with us."[1]

When they reach a green plateau, in front and below are seen the green valley, and on the other side, the mountain rises steeper and harder. The Philanthropist is shocked. He stops and addresses all others, "Here we have come to a decisive turning point. Now the ascent will become steeper, harder and above all, we are going to cross over on to the other side of the mountain where we shall no longer see the valley and the men. This means that I shall have to give up my work and betray my pledge to help humanity. Do not ask me to stay with you."

The Philanthropist is attached to the green valley of life with men, and creatures to serve them, and lull his own ego in disguise. He is considered to be on the lowest rung of the ladder of Integral Yoga and thus is the first man to give up the ascent. The others set out once more leaving the preliminary base, towards the other side. Doubt and absence of faith is a constant companion on the path and draws us back at every stage. The Pessimist is a symbol of faithlessness. He is the second victim who shouts, "We can't even see where we are going! It is an absurdity or a delusion—perhaps both! After all, there might not even be any Truth to discover. The world and life are only a dead end- a hell in which we are imprisoned." It is perhaps the cry of an eternal pessimist who has no chance to go further. He sits there with his head buried in his hands, thus choosing the path of doom.

The third persons to dissociate themselves from the path are the Scientist and the Artist. They are satisfied by the limited and partial aspect of things, due to their own limitations, the truth of their path. To the Scientist, it seems that "We have acted with unpardonable imprudence and our endeavour is not at all scientific." And he hopes that all would finally come back to him in search of a scientific method. Because the path so long followed by them is quite uncertain as each step was not confirmed by experimental verification. The Artist is satisfied with what he has seen so far. He is almost impatient to express the same. For his aim is to express his own subjective experiences in a concrete form.

The Students lack patience and perseverance which is so essential for the spiritual path, for success in each endeavour. As the path becomes narrow, steep and most difficult to scale, the Students want to rest a while though they are somehow aware that "It is always dangerous to delay on the way." But then, they forget that "The path of later on and the road of tomorrow only lead to the castle of nothing at all. "Elsewhere the Mother reminded us: "The one thing quite indispensable is to persevere in the resolve to reach the goal."

So The Students are lost to the rest. Others move on—The Lovers being the last among them, following the rest hand in hand and looking back at the students. While proceeding they find to their left a solitary house facing the infinite sky. All pass but The Lovers stop seeing the marvellous prospect of fulfilment of their individual love. They stay back saying, "We have realised, we two, a perfect, total union, without shadow of cloud. Let us leave the others to their climb to a problematic Truth—we have found our own, our own Truth. That is enough for us."

The sixth one to leave, to remain contented, is The Ascetic. They reach a spot where from nothing is visible above, except a huge rock which rise up like a sheer wall towards the sky so that the summit is out of sight. To the left again, a solitary hut is found, an ideal abode for The Ascetic. The Ascetic declares that he has found his truth, his true being. "I consider that I have reached the end of my path. And here is a sublime and solitary spot, a place that is truly favourable to the life I shall lead from now on. I shall live here in perfect contemplation, far from earth and men, free at last from the need to live." So he departs without a word or a gesture towards the realisation of his personal goal. About this Sri Aurobindo said: "It is this revolt of Spirit against Matter that for two thousand years, since Buddhism disturbed the balance of the old Aryan world, has dominated increasingly the Indian mind . . . . all have lived in the shadow of the great Refusal and the final end of life for all is the garb of the ascetic . . . . renunciation the sole path of knowledge, acceptation of physical life the act of the ignorant, cessation from birth the right use of human birth, the call of the Spirit, the recoil from Matter."[2]

Integral Yoga, the path of Sri Aurobindo and Mother, does not aim at departure from the world for individual salvation. The thing to be done is to bring down the Supramental Consciousness into the earth consciousness for an integral change of life and existence, to establish finally the Life Divine. Sri Aurobindo declared, "Our Yoga is not a retreading of old walks, but a spiritual adventure."[3]

So the aspirants for the ultimate truth do not leave. They valiantly withstand every test and finally reach the summit with a supreme effort. There everything is light, except for the little rock on which they stand, which is hardly big enough for their feet. There they find emptiness, peace, absolute truth everywhere.

The first aspirant admits that to go further they require the intervention of some other power as they have exhausted all possibilities of personal effort. The second aspirant exclaims that Divine grace alone can intervene and perform the miracle. And beyond the horizon they behold another peak resplendent with brilliant light. The promised land, the New Earth! They agree to have absolute trust in Grace, to have absolute faith in the Divine. And indeed they find no other way than to leap from there to the promised land. They leap forward. It is a spiritual adventure. And by the wings of grace they reach the promised land. Looking all around, the second aspirant exclaims, "What marvellous splendour! Now we have only to learn to live the new life." The last part after the leap is the epilogue of the drama, titled "The Realisation."

Notes and References

1. Sri Aurobindo. *The Life Divine*; Chapter III. *Sri Aurobindo Mandir Annual*, 1982. Calcutta; Sri Aurobindo Patha Mandir. p. 30.
2. Sri Aurobindo. *The Life Divine*. Pondicherry; *Sri Aurobindo Birth Centenary Literary*, 1972. V-18. p.23
3. Sri Aurobindo on Himself. Pondicherry; *Sri Aurobindo Birth Centenary Library*, 1972. V- 26. p.109.

12

The Great Secret

The Great Secret is the third drama by the Mother. This might appear to be the least dramatic of the three; yet here too the inner drama is quite at a high pitch. One should never forget that Mother's plays are not just for enjoyment. Her aim was to lead her children to the Golden path, the sunlit path of Truth. It has very little action compared to her other plays. Mother herself accepted it while inviting André to write a part of it.

"For the first December I am preparing something which does not fall into any category of dramatic art and which certainly cannot be called a play . . ." that 'something' is such a compact whole with pulsating language, vibrant with radiating hope, leading towards possible victory, that it may really be called the literature of the future with the unknown young man as the leader.

The play is about six famous men who have reached the peak of human success in their respective field and have been brought together by sheer chance on the way to a world conference on human progress. They are all huddled together in a lifeboat, due to a shipwreck. In this small boat all provisions and water are depleting fast and they all face the inevitable death in the vast and unending ocean. In the beginning the insignificance of all the so-called greatness of men before the vast infinite is portrayed with the simple touch of a great painter's brush. All of them make candid self-assessments foreseeing their imminent end, recapitulate their past and genuinely express their respective feelings of failure in spite of all apparent successes. There is an unknown man at the helm, immobile and silent, who listens to what they say, to utter at last the radiating Truth that really shows them the path as a real solution to all human agonies, dilemmas and problems. Indeed, Mother speaks through the young man.

The play contains six monologues in succession by the six characters and a conclusion by the unknown young man. The six men are The Statesman, The Writer, The Scientist, The Artist, The Industrialist and The Athlete. None of the characters have names; no mention of country or time is made as it is usual with Mother. Here she makes another novel experiment. As the people of the play are from different professions, with their respective mental, vital and physical abilities, their language and expressions cannot be equal. So Mother invited experts in different fields from amongst her disciples to write the monologues of the characters representing their respective faculties. Nolini Kanta Gupta wrote the monologue of the Writer, Pavitra wrote that of the Scientist, Pranab wrote the one of the Athlete and André that of the Industrialist. Mother herself wrote the monologues of the Statesman, the Artist and the unknown young man through whom she spoke.

Though the writers are different Mother (as she had informed in her letter to André) must have edited the different parts to make a harmonious whole, so that it is difficult to realise that the play is not written by the same person. Some excerpts:

"The Statesman relates that helped by his family and personal abilities he had reached the summit of global glory. He tried to go above partisanship and to establish peace, concord, unity among mankind. But in order to establish that he had waged war in spite of all his efforts to the contrary, he confessed that he triumphed finally through unscrupulous means and uncharitable decisions. Though honoured by the whole mankind as 'a friend of humanity', he feels disillusioned and sad and feels he does not deserve the honour.

"I also noticed that success does not really correspond to a person's worth, but rather to his capacity to adapt himself to circumstances and to make himself agreeable. For that, one must flatter people's weakness rather than attempt to correct their imperfectness."

The Writer, throughout his life, experimented with words. Like a juggler he had played around with their meaning and usage. His creations were vast and varied. They ranged from lyrical poetry to legends, parables, episodes, plays, novels and biographies, culminating in an awe inspiring grand epic. He combined in himself all the great masters of literature scattered through various countries and ages. Yet he feels that he has not been able to grasp the truth of things, nor the beauty of their soul. He has scratched only the surface. He remains dissatisfied, unhappy. His conclusion is "Dreams have I sown in the air."

The Scientist saw the birth of the atom bomb and discovered the process of obtaining electric power directly from nuclear energy that brought about a radical change in the economic conditions of the world. He has achieved super excellence in his field and has been honoured. He discovered the process of separating atom not only from uranium but from other base, common metals. But he is in a great dilemma as to whether to make his new discovery known to the world. The horror of the atom bomb and the hydrogen bomb makes him hesitant about declaring his discovery to mankind that is capable of being unscrupulous. "We have reached a point where, unless there is a rapid and radical moral change, mankind will destroy itself with the power it has in its own hands."

He too is not certain about the truth: "One always has the impression of circling around the truth, the reality, of approaching it from different angles and from different points of view, without being able to discover it or grasp it. Nor does it spring forth and reveal itself . . . . On the shores of the Infinite, I discovered a footprint and I sought to reconstruct the being which had left its mark on the sands. I succeeded at last and found that it was myself."

The Artist feels that he has been a complete failure in terms of his high ideals in spite of his success as a world renowned artist. "My conception of genius is quite different. We have to create new forms, with new methods and processes, in order to express a new kind of beauty that is higher and purer, truer and nobler. So long as I still feel bound to human animality, I cannot free myself completely from the forms of material nature." The aspiration was there, but the knowledge, the vision was lacking.

The Industrialist has created important organisations; mass producing cars, creating employment, riches, raising the standard of living of man not only in his own country but also, in other countries. But at the end of it all a big question looms before him. "What have I contributed to humanity." He has increased desires and greeds and jealousies in mankind. "I feel that there is a secret yet to be discovered; and without this of discovery all our efforts are in vain."

The Athlete has achieved worldwide fame. As a sportsman he has achieved the highest physical perfection, has been awarded innumerable prizes. He is recognised as an expert throughout the world and yet he is at a loss to discover the utility and purpose of all this.

When all is said and an uneasy calm dwells, the voice of the unknown young man is heard; calm, gentle and clear with serene authority: "What you want to know, I can tell you." They listen spellbound. The young man continues:

"None of you have found the solution, for this riddle of life cannot be solved by mental man, however superior he may be. For that, one must be born into a new and higher consciousness, the Truth-consciousness. For behind these fleeting appearances there is an eternal reality, behind this unconscious and warring multitude there is a single, serene consciousness, behind these endless and innumerable falsehoods there is a pure, radiant Truth, behind this obscure and obdurate ignorance there is a sovereign knowledge."

Then he explains that this sovereign reality is very clear, at the centre of our being. This is to be attained and lived. And for this we are not to shun the world but to embrace it. Through it we have to proceed with ardent faith and aspiration, and surrender. In fact the whole of nature is slowly proceeding towards that evolution. We can accelerate it through our will, work and aspiration. Here he also describes bow matter has been evolving slowly from inanimate objects towards Supramental Consciousness.

The time has come for this possibility, promised and anticipated so long, to become a living reality upon earth, and that is why you are all unsatisfied and feel that you have been unable to attain what you wanted from *life*.

The unknown young man continues to speak and there comes an inner change in the others. They exchange glances. The Writer admits that a new possibility, new horizon is before them but, "Alas, it is too late.

The unknown young man unmoving, declares, "No, it is not too late, it is never too late. Let us unite our wills in a great aspiration; let us pray for an intervention of the grace. A miracle can always happen."

After some time they all concentrate and following the young man, pray in a united voice to the "Supreme Reality to reveal his marvellous secret. After a pause The Artist exclaims, "Look! Look!"

A ship which appeared like a dot in the horizon slowly comes closer. The Athlete jumps up into the gunwale and waves a white handkerchief. The ship comes nearer, to their rescue. All are vibrant with a new hope of life, a new horizon. The unknown man says slowly: "Here is salvation, here is new life!"

We may remember that the *Ascent to Truth* ended with the same words, "Now we have only to learn to live the new life." So in *Towards the Future* the couple and She, all "took a leap towards the future, a new life."

Work Cited

On Education. Part-3; Dramas. The Mother. Collected Works. Centenary Edition. 1978. Pondicherry; Sri Aurobindo Ashram. pp. 473-518.

Short Stories

13

Part One

A favourite medium of the mother's teaching was through simple stories. She narrated many such stories in her Wednesday classes which were taken from her own life or of those known to her, and from many other sources to teach the children. Besides the classes her talks at different times were full of stories. These stories may be divided into three groups: those which were facts, incidents she had witnessed or incidents from her own life, those she adapted and translated from different sources and lastly, those she wrote as stories, products of her imagination.

We shall first discuss the stories of the second group, i.e., those which are adaptations and translations. Many of these stories and fables include treasures of the world. They move from country to country, language to language through the enthusiastic scholars of different ages. Such are the tales of the *Panchatantra*, *Aesop's Fables*, stories from the *Jataka*, stories from the *Ramayana* and the *Mahabharata* and so on. lswar Chandra Vidyasagar, the notable educationist of Bengal, a pioneer of modern Bengali education and culture, adapted many of *Aesop's Fables* into Bengali for young students.

Mother, during her stay in Japan, translated and adapted several stories from E.J. Gould's stories. Her version of the stories written in French were first published under the title *Belles Histoires* in 1946. Subsequently its English version was published in 1951 as *Tales of All Times.* In a statement in 1950 Mother said that the stories had been written to help the young ones to discover themselves and to discover the path of truth and beauty. The stories were grouped under eleven main qualities such as 'Self Control', 'Courage', 'Cheerfulness', etc.

There were some more unpublished stories arranged under five more attributes. These were 'The Giver', 'The Conquest of Knowledge', 'Modesty', 'The Family' and 'Sympathy' which were for the first time printed as Appendix of *Tales of All Times* in *The Mother's Collected Works*, Vol. 2, *Words of long ago.* Some of the stories have been translated into other languages.

Incidents and characters in the stories belong to different parts of the world. But most of them are from India. Many are from Arabia and Persia. The stories are from epics, legends, myths, history, fables and other sources. Each group, often described as a garland of pearls and other gems, contains an introduction followed by small stories interposed by Mother's remarks. They are appeals to the children to follow the golden path with a concluding comment at the end. The groups do not contain equal number of stories. Sometimes the part played by stories is negligible, as in *'order* group.' At times it is the description of a picture which Mother picks up as sufficient food for thought and lesson.

The Japanese have a picturesque way of expressing their ideas on prudence. They have in one of their temples an image of the meditating Buddha seated on a lotus. In front of him are three little monkeys, one with its hands over its eyes, another over its ears and the third covering its mouth. What do these three monkeys signify? By its gesture the first one implies: "I do not see evil." The second one says: "I do not hear it." And the third, "I do not speak it." Similarly, the wise man is prudent about what he looks at, what he listens to, and what he says.

Let us narrate a few of her stories under different groups as samples of the gems with which her garlands are made.

Self Control: Hussain was the grandson of Prophet Mohammed. His home was beautiful and his purse well filled. Whoever offended him offended a rich man, and heavy is the anger of the rich.

One day a slave carrying a bowl of boiling hot water was passing by Hussain as he dined. By misfortune a little water fell upon the grandson of the Prophet who let out a cry of rage.

Falling to his knees, the slave had this presence of mind to recall an appropriate verse of the Quran:

Paradise is for those who bridle their anger he said.... "And for those who forgive men," continued the slave. "I forgive you" said Hussain.

". . . . For Allah loves the merciful, the servant added: (In the course of this exchange Hussain's anger had vanished. Now wholly at peace with himself he made the slave rise and said:

"From now on you are free. Here take these four hundred pieces of silver."

In this way Hussain learnt how to bridle his temper which was as generous as it was hasty. Since his noble character was neither wicked nor cruel, it was worthy of being controlled.

In the introduction it was stated that a horse, however wild it might be, can be bridled, but with a tiger it is never possible, as the animal is wicked by nature. So, human character, Mother says, can also be bridled by self control.

Abu Otman al-Hiri was known for his excessive patience. One day he was invited to a feast but when arrived he was told, "You must excuse me, I cannot receive you. So please go back home and may Allah have mercy on you." No sooner did he arrive home than he was again invited by his friend and again the same reply was received after reaching his house. Four times the same act was repeated. At last he was received and was told that his patience was being tested. When praised, Abu Otman said, "Don't praise me, for dogs practise the same virtue, they come when they are called and go when they are sent away." Was it a virtue at all, this meekness? Here is the conclusion: Did then this man who was so meek had nothing in him to control? Oh, yes he had! It was the most difficult thing of all to control the weakness of his character. And yet it was because he did not know how to control himself that everyone controlled him as they pleased.

Mother profusely commends the noble work of Babu Pratap Chandra Roy who took great pains throughout his life to get the Sanskrit *Mahabharata* translated into English, and presented it the English reading public for the first time. Even during his lifetime the whole work could not be completed but on his deathbed he said to his wife, "The book must be completed. Don't spend money on my funeral rites if it is needed for the printing. Live as simply as you can so as to save money for the *Mahabharata*." His faithful wife followed his instructions and the book in 11 volumes was presented to the European readers. At the end the Mother addresses children of the country,

"And you, brave children, will you not join the great army of men and women who never tire of doing good and never abandon their task until they have completed it?"

And what is perseverance? Perseverance is an active patience, a patience that marches on. The sustained energy and the unremitting will that we call perseverance. To give an example, she tells the story of the famous sage, *Shankaracharya* who lived some 1,200 years ago and who had resolved during his childhood to become a sannyasi. His mother opposed and the boy could not disobey her.

One day mother and child went to bathe in a river. Shankara dived in and felt his foot suddenly siezed by a crocodile. Death seemed close at hand. But even at that dreadful moment the brave child thought only of his great project and cried out to his mother, "I am lost! A crocodile is dragging me down. But let me at least die as a sannyasi!" "Yes, yes, my son, his mother sobbed in despair. Shankara felt such joy that he had found the strength to free his foot and threw himself ashore.

Mother gave the example of Columbus, the explorer and Palissy, the potter, who could not have achieved what they did without the double virtue of patience and perseverance. We add the modern example of Mihir Sen, the sea-explorer. K. R. S. Iyengar added the name of M. V. Ramanujachari to this list relating to the Tamil *Mahabharata* in his book, *On the Mother*.

Simple Life: The Mother is a great advocate of such a life. She blessed all those who followed a simple life. "In every age," she said, "the best and most energetic survivors of earth's progress have known how to lead a quiet and frugal life, which keeps the body in good health and enables man to take a more active part in working for the common good. Their example will always put to shame all those who pile up useless treasures and become slaves to their vast quantities of servants, clothes and furniture." Then she made a sudden illuminating comment which would otherwise satisfy the political philosophers of the left leaning. Nevertheless, it remains a truth for all ages, "You cannot make a heap without making a hole," and too often the luxury of some represents the poverty of many others.

Mother brings the example of Prophet Mohammed who professes drinking wine and gambling to be a sin. Therefore all who respect the Quran do not drink or gamble, and they are profited. Mother quickly adds, with innocent sarcasm, "But on the other hand there are many good people all over the world who find it right to take spirits. We respect their opinions. But these same people cannot assert that it is wrong not to take alcohol."

Prudence: A merchant of the ancient city of Benaras helped two vultures in their miserable condition. The vultures, after being cured and regaining their health, flew away but remembered the kind help of the merchant with gratitude. Now they in turn began to pick up all the garments from people's houses in cities and villages, and dropped them into the house of the good merchant. The merchant could understand the act of gratitude but kept all the garments intact without using them. When one of the vultures was caught and brought to the court, it confessed everything and the merchant in turn admitted it and was ready to return all the clothes. Although the bird acted without discernment, the king pardoned both for their gratitude and prudence.

On the other side there is the famous story of imprudence of prince Dasharatha of Ayodhya who, out of over confidence in his archery, being a *Sadabhedi*, killed the only son of a blind hermit and his wife. In consequence he had to suffer the loss of his beloved son Ramachandra, exiled for 14 years on the day of his coronation.

Sincerity is the group under which Mother has brought forth the largest number of stories from all sources. Sincerity is the presiding deity of her story, "The Virtues," to be discussed later. Of these stories mention may be made of the story of four princes of Benaras. All of them wanted to see the *Kimshuka* tree. They were accordingly taken at different times by the charioteer to the jungle and the desired tree was shown. One day, when the four brothers were together, someone asked "What does the *Kimsuka,* tree look like?

The eldest said, "Like a bare trunk."

The second, "Like a flourishing banana tree."

The third, "Like a pink and red bouquet."

and the Fourth, "Like an acacia laden with fruit."

Unable to agree, they went to their father. The king smiled and said: "All four of you are right, but all four of you forget that the tree is not the same in all seasons."

The story resembles the story of the blind person's idea about the elephant. Mother commented that in this way, most often, men know only a fraction of the truth, and their error comes precisely from the fact that they think they know it all. "How much less this error would be if they had learnt at an early age to love truth so much that they would always seek it more and more."

After telling the stories, Mother said to the children: "Little children, the world is full of superstitions, and the best means given to men to discover more of the truth is to remain always sincere and to become always more so in thought, deed and word; for it is when we avoid deceiving others in all things that we also learn to deceive ourselves less and less."

In the family group Mother started with animals, telling them about the love and affection between the ewe and lamb, and ended with the filial love of the white elephant and its old mother. In between she went through many stories and elaborated her definitions with human beings at the centre.

"So in our idea of the family let us include father, mother, child, brother, sister, grandparents, servants and the animals that help man. Of course, the ways and customs of families are not the same in every country of the world . . . . But in all of them, love rules in their hearts and affection is the law."

Mother's first group of stories are those that she narrated while talking and replying questions. These are true stories, coming out of her own adventures and rich experiences during the different periods of her life. They were stories that originated in different contexts at different places in the world. Many of them are really humorous and would make an interesting book.

Those who have read the life of Mother from her childhood, have enjoyed a number of stories, such as how once her feet had slipped in the mountain at Fontainebleau and how miraculously she was saved. Or how she, in anger, once lifted a 13-year-old bully, as he was teasing the younger girls, and threw him down on the ground with a thud. Or how when she used to play the piano, a big frog would sit in a corner, appreciating her music and would "quack" the moment she stopped playing as a gesture of disapproval. Again as she played, it would stop and listen attentively. When in Algiers, she was meditating in a forest, a big venomous cobra hissed angrily as she was obstructing its way by sitting on its abode. However, Mother looked straight at the snake. The snake could not bear the force of her sight for long and had soon to retreat in the nearby pool. These incidents apart, we are quoting a few interesting stories as told by her on different occasions (Titles ours).

Expression of Love in the Desire to be Devoured: "It is also said that the first expression of love in living beings is the desire to devour. One wants to absorb, desires to devour. There is one instance which would seem to prove that this is not altogether false, that is when the tiger catches its prey or the snake its victim, it happens that both the tiger's and the snake's victims give themselves up in a kind of delight of being eaten. An experience is narrated of a man who was in the bush with his friends and had lagged behind and was caught by a tiger, a man-eater. When the others came back they saw that he was missing. They saw the tracks. They ran after him, just in time to prevent the tigers eating him. When he came to himself a little, they told him that he must have had a frightful experience. He said: "No just imagine, I don't know what had happened to me as soon as that tiger caught me and while it was dragging me along, I felt an intense love for it and a great desire to be eaten by it?"

"This is quite true, it is not an invention. It is a true story. Well, I have seen with my own eyes . . . . It was in the cage in the *Jardin Des Planetes* in Paris. It was the breakfast day. I happened to be there. The cage was opened, the little white rabbit put inside. It was a pretty little white rabbit and it immediately fled to the other end of the cage and trembled like anything. It was horrible to see this, for it knew very well what was happening, it had felt the snake, it knew very well. The serpent was simply coiled up on its mat. It seemed to be asleep, and very quietly it stretched out its neck and head, and then began looking at the rabbit. It looked at it without stirring—just looked at it. I saw the rabbit which at first stopped trembling; it no longer was afraid. It was quite doubled up and it began to recover. And then I saw it lift its head, open its eyes wide, and look at the snake, and slowly, very slowly it went forward towards it till it was just at the right distance. Then the snake with a single leap—without any disturbance, without even uncoiling itself, just remaining where it was, you understand—hop! it took it, began rolling it, preparing it for its dinner. It crushed all its bones nicely, made them crack; then it smeared it with a kind of gluey substance to make it quite snippy. And when it was all quite ready, it began swallowing it, slowly, comfortably . . . . But it didn't have to disturb itself, it was the other creature that had come to it.

"There you are. Indeed there are many things in nature". (Talk on 8 July 1953)

Vampires Active During the First World War: "It was in Japan. It was the beginning of January, 1919. Anyway, it was the time when a terrible flu raged there in the whole of Japan, which killed hundreds of thousands of people. It was one of those epidemics the like of which is rarely seen. In Tokyo, every day there were hundreds and hundreds of new cases. The disease appeared to take this turn; it lasted three days and on the third day the patient died . . . . If one did not die on the third day, at the end of seven days one was altogether cured. There was a panic in the town.

"I was living with someone who never ceased troubling me. 'But what is this disease? What is there behind this disease?' I was simply to cover myself with my force, my protection, so as not to catch it.

"One day I was called to the other end of the town.... I was in the tram and seeing these people with masks on their noses, and then there was in the atmosphere this constant fear....

"I began to ask myself: 'Truly, what is this illness? What is there behind this illness?'

"I came to the house . . . . I had caught it. It came to you thus, without preparation, instantaneously . . . . Well, that evening I had a terrible fever. The doctor was called (it was not I who called him) . . . and he told me, 'I must absolutely give you this medicine.' It was one of the best medicines for the fever, he had just a little (all their stocks were exhausted, everyone was taking it); he said: 'I have still a few packets, I shall give you some'. 'I beg of you, do not give it to me. I won't take it. Keep it for someone who has faith in it and will take it.' He was quite disgusted: 'It was no use of my coming here.' So I said: 'Perhaps it was no use!' And I remained in my bed, with my fever, a violent fever . . . . At the end of the second day, as I was lying all alone, I saw clearly a being, with a part of the head cut off, in a military uniform (or the remains of a military uniform) approaching me and suddenly flinging himself upon my chest . . . to suck my force. I took a good look, then realised that I was about to die. He was drawing all my life out (for I must tell you that people were dying of pneumonia in three days). I was completely nailed to the bed, without movement, in a deep trance. I could no longer stir and he was pulling. I thought: now it is the end. Then I called on my occult power, I gave a big fight and I succeeded in turning him back so that he could not stay there any longer. And I woke up.

"But I had seen. And I had learnt. I had understood that the illness originated from the beings who had been thrown out of their bodies. I had seen this during the First Great War, towards its end ... they were turned into so many countless vampires. And they vampirised upon men.... I know how much knowledge and force were necessary for me to resist. It was irresistible."

"I passed two or three days absolutely quiet, in concentration, with my consciousness. Subsequently a friend of ours (a Japanese, a very good friend) came and told me: 'Ah.

You are ill? So what I thought was true . . . . Just imagine for the last two or three days, there hasn't been a single new case of illness in the town and most of the people who were ill have been cured and the number of deaths has become almost negligible, and now it is all over. The illness is wholly under control.' Then I narrated what had happened to me and he went and narrated it to everybody. They even published articles about it in the papers." (Talk of 22 July 1953)

Catastrophic Vision

"An American gentleman had arrived at one of those big American hotels where there are lifts; now, early in the morning just before getting up, he had a dream which he remembered well; he had seen a boy dressed as a lift-boy and making the same movements a lift-boy makes directing you to get in. He was there. And then, at the end of the movement, instead of a lift there was a hearse! - that is to say, that kind of carriage. Oh! You must have seen somewhere now and then, to carry the dead to the cemetry; when they are not burnt, they are carried on a bier with black draperies etc. So there was such a carriage, a hearse for carrying the dead. And the boy was singing to him to get into the carriage.

"When he came out of his room, the boy was there with the lift to take him down; exactly the same boy, the same face, the same dress, the same gesture. He remembered the hearse—he did not get into the lift. He said, 'No, No!" and he walked down. And before he reached the ground floor he heard a terrible noise and the lift crashed down to the ground and all who were in it were killed. It was because of the dream that he had not got in, for he had understood. Therefore in such a case when you have the vision, you can avert the catastrophe." (Talk 29 July, 1953)

What Happens When One Eats Meat?

"I will tell you a story. I know a young Swedish woman who was doing *sadhana*. Normally she was a vegetarian by habit as well as by inclination. One day she was invited to a dinner. She was given fowl to eat. She did not like to make a fuss and quietly ate her fowl. Now at night she found herself, in dream of course, in a basket and her head in between two bits of sticks and being shaken, shaken to and fro. She felt very unhappy, very miserable. And then she saw herself head down and legs up in the air and being shaken, shaken continually, she was thoroughly miserable. All on a sudden she felt she was being skinned, peeled and how painful it all was! And then someone came with a knife and cut off her head. She woke up at that. She told me the story and said that she had never had such a frightful nightmare in her life. She had thought nothing of this kind before going to bed; it must have been simply the consciousness of the poor chicken that entered into her and she experienced in—dream all the agonies of the creature when it was being taken to the market—her feathers pulled out and in the end head severed. That is what happens. In other words, along with the meal that you take, you absorb also, in large or small measure, the consciousness of the animal whose flesh you swallow." (Talk of 23 June 1954)

Now I shall now discuss the third group of her stories that should actually be called the first group, not only because those were written earlier but also because those are the original stories written by Mother. Sri Aurobindo also wrote four stories. The four stories by the Mother are—*The Path of Later On, The Virtues, A Saphire Tale* and *A Leader*. The last one was based on real incidance.

The Path of Later On was written by her when she was 15 years old and a school student in 1893. The story starts on a happy note. A young traveller walks happily under the morning sun with many-coloured flowers greeting him on both sides of the road. But after a while he comes to a crossroad where many paths branched off in all directions. Here the traveller is in a dilemma. He wonders which road to follow. All of us in our lives must have, at least once, come to such a crossroad where everything dependeds on our decision at that crucial hour: 'Which road to take?' However, the young man takes the easy path full of birds, flowers and lovely grass and seems comfortable. But somewhere inside, he feels he has not chosen the right path. A voice seems to tell him, "Turn back, turn back. You are not on the right road." But the attractive present prevents him. He defers his decision supported by the surrounding. 'Later on' 'Later on' he says and proceeds. 'Do not be misled by indolence and weakness; do not fall asleep in the present; come to the future, voices warn him but the young man goes on. Gradually the sun sets; the charming road leads to stony, dusty, rocky ravines where human figures roll. Hollow voices cry out. 'Flee this place; go back to the crossroads; still there is time.' But alas! It is perhaps too late. The young man hesitates and then replies, 'Tomorrow'. The sun disappears, all around him are deserts. The desperate traveller knocks against phantoms. All around him is ruins. He hears stifled cries and stumbles on skeletons. He tries to close his eyes. At last he comes before a dark, desolate, gloomy castle. Thinking that he has reached his goal, as he tries to enter, the whole edifice crumbles down turning into dust. Owls, crows, bats fly out circling round his head. Horrible phantoms who bear the names of Desolation, Despair, Disgust and Suicide, surround him and draw him towards the abyss. He feels hypnotized.

"When the traveller is at the edge of the gulf, all his efforts prove to be in vain. After a supreme struggle "he falls.... from his bed."

Mother stuns us with a whip-crack ending but it is towards a better end. Although we are stunned, we laugh after a while, when we learn that the young traveller is a student who, having lots of tasks in hand, feeling a little tired retired early to bed to do everything the next morning. The boy admits to himself- the path is called 'the path of later on,' the road is the 'road of tomorrow' and the great building, the "castle of nothing at all". He at once sets to work 'vowing to himself that he would never put off until tomorrow what he could do today.'

This is the lesson of the story, the lesson that all responsible and great men teach us. But we have to remember that Mother was only a girl when she wrote it. We also note the Aurobindonian futuristic call, "Do not fall asleep in the present; come to the future," was given by the Mother, who was to translate this ideal in her life and in the lives of humanity of the future.

The Virtues is a symbolic story which has no root on this earth, so is not directly related to us. It is about a conference of gods and goddesses to be held in a palace which stood on a very high cloud. The conference was to be held in the Hall of Intelligence where, near the ground the light was very soft; it became saphire-blue, clearer towards the ceiling. What is most interesting about the story is its lucid, straightforward style, which makes everything crystal-clear.

The gods and goddesses assembled and were honoured by the mortals by the symbolic name of their virtues. They were named *Sincerity, Humility, Modesty, Courage, Charity, Solicitude* and others. The short description that Mother gave about them and about their surrounding made it clear what the virtues actually mean. *Sincerity,* the presiding deity, was dressed in a transparent robe, like clear water, and held in her hand a cube of purest crystal, through which things could be seen as they really were, far different from what they usually seemed, for there, their image was reflected without distortion (Sincerity actually means that.) So, *Courage* too, lofty-browed, clear-eyed, his lips firm and smiling with a calm and resolute air. *Humility,* both respectful and dignified. However, they were the divine personalities who usually live scattered in different worlds. Their meeting was a rare occasion.

After everyone had come, a newcomer appeared at the golden threshold. There was nothing impressive in her appearance. She was very young and slight, and the white dress she wore was very simple, poor. After a long hesitation she was allowed entrance by the guards. And after entering she felt very shy in that elegant assembly as they listened. She was *Gratitude.*

A Leader

He was asked to think deeply and calmly with retrospect. That's when a few books on the Mother's ideas and her group came into their hands. Her practical and pragmatic ideas attracted them. As a result the group sent their leader to Paris to seek guidance from her.

At the beginning there was no proper communication between the newcomer, the fugitive, and Mother's group. His clothes were clean but worn out, his arms were held close to his sides. His face was pale and half concealed beneath a black hat. Even when he greeted the Mother's group they could not distinguish the features of his waxen face. In reply to questions about his occupation, the man replied, "I work for the revolution. "The reply sounded like a knell amid the luxury of this bourgeois apartment. However, at last there was full amity and they understood each other. The man admitted that to win freedom, a nation should deserve it, prepare itself to enjoy it. Russia was not ready at that time, so the masses were to be educated and pulled out of torpor. Mother advised him to shun the path of violence. "How can you hope to win justice with injustice, harmony with hatred?"

The man readily admitted that she was right. He profusely thanked her having taken such a keen interest in their cause despite being a woman. At the same time he admitted with deep gratitude the selfless help that was rendered to him by a woman of his country. Defying her own safety and security Mother and her group wanted to help him and invited him another day. The man readily accepted saying, "It is good to meet people one can trust, people who have the same ideal of justice as we have and do not look upon us as criminals or lunatics because we want to realise it. Good bye! . . . ." The man admitted that even in Paris he was closely spied on and that he had no peace. The story ends:

"He never returned. He excused himself in a hastily written note. Too closely watched, under suspicion, tracked down after he had changed his lodgings many times, this gentle, just man had to return to his own country; a terrible country where perhaps a tragic end awaited him . . . ."

The end is touching and tragic. We feel moved and sympathise with the revolutionary. Somewhere in the depth of our heart we pray for the victory of the revolutionary.

Works Cited

Words of Long Ago. The Mother. Collected Works. Centenary Edition. Pondicherry; Sri Aurobindo Ashram. 1978. V-2

The Mother: Questions and Answers; different volumes.

14

Part Two

Mother's Sapphire Tale

Originally written in French, *Conte Saphire*, a short story, was written in October 1906 and was published for the first time with an English rendering as *A Saphire Tale* in Mother India in its February 1957 issue.

Except the *Path of Later On, The Saphire Tale and The Virtues* her other stories were facts taken from real life or adapted from other works. *A Saphire Tale* is her imaginative work, one of the most outstanding of her stories, a fine romantic creation. It does not deal with a particular period or country. It starts quite traditionally:

"Once upon a time, far away in the East, there was a small country that lived in order and harmony, where each one in his own place played the part for which he was made, for the greatest good of all."

"Each one tried to contribute his best for the common good. There were workmen, artists, scientists, philosophers, guiding the state and the king. The king was king because he was the most intelligent and he alone was capable of fulfilling the needs of everyone. "

Now this is like an ideal kingdom. The ideals referred to has been mentioned later by the Mother in her *Charter for Auroville.* Except for the king, who represents a bygone age, the ideal applies to all. However, the king here was more than 200 years old and though otherwise fit, he wanted to retire. So he called his son Meotha. Meotha too was another exemplary personality who grew up with all fine qualities and was loved universally in the kingdom. So there was no dispute about his inheriting the throne.

"But as you know, "the king said," according to the age old custom, no one may ascend the throne unless he is united by bonds of integral affinity with one who can bring him peace and equilibrium by a perfect match of tastes and abilities. "The prince admitted that he had not so far been able to find such a match in the kingdom. He requested the king to permit him to go out for a year to foreign countries in order to get himself acquainted with the laws and customs of those countries and also find his match, if possible. The king blessed his son and gave his permission.

The second part of the story is enacted on an island, again unnamed. "Amid the Western Ocean lies a little island valued for its valuable forests. There, under the trees, in the woods, walks slowly on a radiant summer's day a young girl named Liane. Her body is graceful. lips carmine, hair so golden that it shines and her eyes are like two deep doors opening on a limitless blue, which light up her features with their intellectual radiance. In a dream she has seen a man, who seems from his dress, to have come from a distant land and to whom the girl has given herself totally. For him she waits. To her the forests and birds and the whole atmosphere are quite friendly and sympathetic. She is an orphan. We remember Kalidasa's Shakuntala, a unique creation, who has some resemblance to Liane.

Liane is walking in complete silence under the thick foliage of the wood which cannot be pierced even by the dazzling sunlight. She is walking in a half dream, expectant. "Suddenly a bird's song rings out clear and joyful; all uneasiness vanishes . . . ." She is seized by an emotion of great sweetness, all appears beautiful and good to her, and tears come to her eyes, it seems to her that the trees quivering in the breeze, the moss rustling beneath her feet, the bird renewing its melody—all speak to her of the One whom she awaits.

She trembles with emotion in the expectation of meeting the beloved, presses her hands against her beating heart and now the sensation grows intense. "Liane opens her eyes sure of a presence. Oh, wonder of wonders! He is there, he, he in truth as she has seen him in her dream . . . more handsome than men usually are—It was Meotha."

They look at each other in a supreme joy of rediscovery. They recognise that they have known each other in the distant past. Liane calmly comes and places her hand in the hand he offers her and they wend their way through the forest—"Silent in a silence filled with thoughts exchanged." A great ship comes near the shore and a boat comes to take them to the ship. Liane trustingly, meekly follows Meotha. Then as the ship glides and the little island disappears below the horizon, the girl speaks:

I was waiting for you, and now that you have come, I have followed you without question. We are made for each other. I feel it, I know it . . . . I would like to know to what shore you are taking me."

As he reciprocates the feelings of Liane and tells her where he is taking her to be his queen, we may imagine Meotha soliloquising:

> With life for ever old yet new,
> Changed not in kind but in degree,
> The instant made eternity,
> And heaven just prove that 1 and she
> Ride, ride together, for ever ride?[1]

The situation created in the story may be said to be Lovers' Paradise. Meotha and Liane, it appears, seems to know each other from births immemorial. They wait on earth for the opportune moment only. It looks as if the story floated on the light wings of imagination and the lovers met very easily without the usual pang of separation that may lead to real happiness in union. But is not their living apart a deep enough sorrow to find a proper bliss of union when they meet? In fact their joy of surrender and acceptance, the rapture of union is something beyond the grasp of the ordinary. The story is created on an occult level and here the lovers' lives are like open pages. When they meet silently and glide together, even before they speak, it seems many untold stories are told. And we have to relish the story in the deep silence of our heart. For we realise its meaning better through our heart than through our intelligence.

The Mother is always for this ideal love where lovers meet in a deeper urge than mere likes and dislikes and often love before they see each other physically as the Poet and Clairvoyant in Mother's drama *Towards the Future.*

"The story embodies, Mother said to the Editor of *Mother India,* The ideal of an Overmind Creation."

To understand this better we may quote a few passages from the Mother and Sri Aurobindo. While answering some questions Mother said:

"Sri Aurobindo has called the Supermind the world of Truth. But in between is what he has distinguished as the Overmind, the world of the Cosmic Gods. Now it is this Overmind that has up to the present governed our world: it is the highest that man has been able to attain in illumined consciousness."[2]

And Sri Aurobindo, while discussing the Overmind creation in literature, remarked:

"You must remember that the Overmind is a Superhuman Consciousness and to be able to write always or purely from an Overmind inspiration would mean the elevation of at least a part of the nature beyond the human level."

"But how do you expect a Supramental inspiration to come down here when the Overmind itself is so rarely within human reach?"[3]

The Mother continues in the same discourse as already cited: "No doubt, the Supermind has also acted in the history of the world but always through the Overmind. It is the direct descent of the Supramental Consciousness and Power that alone can utterly re-create life in terms of the Spirit. For, in the Overmind there is already the play of possibilities which marks the beginning of this lower triple world of Mind, Life and Matter in which we have our existence. And whenever there is this play and not the spontaneous and infallible working of the innate Truth of the Spirit, there is the seed of distortion and ignorance. Not that the Overmind is a field of ignorance; but it is the border-line between the Higher and the Lower, for, the play of possibilities, of separate even if not yet divided choice, is likely to lead to deviation from the Truth of things."[4]

And Sri Aurobindo in *The Life' Divine says:* "Purusha and Prakriti, Conscious Soul and executive Force of Nature, are in the supramental harmony a two-aspected single truth, being the dynamis of the Reality; there can be no disequilibrium or predominance of one over the other. In Overmind we have the origin of the cleavage."[5]

Having understood that the Supramenral Consciousness is the Truth-Consciousness and the Overmental creation a derivation from the Supramental and that a cleavage commences from it, we shall present Mother's views about the two which are relevant for our present purpose.

On the 10 July 1957 Mother related a very interesting story from her life. In 1926 after Sri Aurobindo had retired for his *sadhana* for the Supramental Manifestation: Mother assumed charge of the Ashram and thereafter—

"Things took a certain shape: a very brilliant creation was worked out in extraordinary detail, with marvellous experiences, contacts with divine beings and all kinds of manifestations which are considered miraculous."[6]

One day she went as usual to relate to Sri Aurobindo what had been happening. Sri Aurobindo said to her: "Yes, this is an Overrnind creation. It is very interesting, very well done. You will perform miracles which will make you famous throughout the world . . . .

"It will be a great success. But it is an Overmind creation. And it is not the success that we want; we want to establish the Supermind on earth. One must know how to renounce immediate success in order to create the new world, the Supramental World in its integrality."[7]

Mother realised the meaning of his words and a few hours later the creation was gone.

On the same date Mother related another of her experiences. She was watching a Bengali film *Rani Rashmoni* where Sri Ramakrishna, the temple of Dakshineswar, the statue of Kali were all being shown. While seeing the film

Mother suddenly realised that though the relations with God, the ideals of oneness of all religions, etc. were there in it as they were the purest and the highest spiritual effort of man, it was a world that had ceased to be real. It was transcended and surpassed by something which was only beginning to express itself. Obviously, Mother was referring to the descent of the Supramental Consciousness and force on the 29 February 1956 on earth. She was extremely emphatic about the ultimate victory of the Supermind as visioned by Sri Aurobindo.

"The old world, the creation of what Sri Aurobindo calls the Overmind, was an age of the gods and consequently the age of religions . . . .

"In the Supramental creation there will no longer be any religions. The whole life will be the expression, the flowering into forms of the divine Unity manifesting in the world. And there will no longer be what men now call gods."[8]

On the 15 May 1957 someone had asked, "Since the beginning of creation why is there this difference between the male and the female?"

Mother forcibly stated that it was not true. She said it was so only in the material world, that too not wholly. Neither in the vital nor in the mental world is this distinction a 'must'.

"Now, there are many people who are very keen on this distinction—they may keep it if they like!—but it is not at all something final or eternal ... or perfect in itself. It was perhaps the ideal of Overmind creation, that is possible ... and yet, even then not totally, only partially. But still those who are so fond of this differentiation—let them keep it if they like! If it gives them pleasure ... It has its advantages and disadvantages, many disadvantages."[9]

The Supramental Manifestation was perhaps a dream in 1906 when the present story was written. In the meantime what had been promised was fulfilled, and with the Supramental manifestation, in whatever small way or limited sphere, Mother visualised, at least symbolically, that the age of the old world was gone and that the Supramental had taken the field. Still, as she and Sri Aurobindo said, it is not expected that all will be supramentalised in no time. Aeons may pass before such a divine plan actually comes to fruition, depending on many things. Both the old world and the new creation will continue. Mother was not for the old world, the world of separative religions, the world of the male and the female. So she said in 1957 that the story was "The ideal of an Overmind creation." Short of the Supramental, it is the purest and noblest ideal that man has so far created and with the present mental, vital and physical stature of mankind, the Overmental creation is the highest conceivable. The story of love between Liane and Meotha is thus an ideal one that we may cherish in our hearts.

Notes and References

1. From Robert Browning's "The last ride together".
2. *The Mother. Collected Works.* Pondichcrry; Sri Aurobindo Ashram. V- 3. p.173.
3. Sri Aurobindo. *The Future Poetry.* Pondicherry; SABCL. 1 972. V-9. p.370.
4. *The Mother.* V- 3. pp.173-174.
5. Sri Aurobindo. *The Life Divine.* Pondicherry; SABCL. V-18. p. 279.
6. *The Mother.* V-9. p.148.
7. *The Mother.* p.148.
8. *Ibid.* pp.149-150.
9. *Ibid.* p.10.

15

Mother's Words

Before we begin with Mother's words let us see what she said about the Word itself.

"Words are words. After all, they mean nothing, unless there is something behind. Have you never noticed that when you speak to certain people, you may express yourself quite clearly and yet they understand nothing: and to others you say just two words and they understand immediately? . . . it does not depend upon the external form, the words one speaks, but on the force of the thought one puts into them; and the greater, stronger, more precise and clear the thought-force, the more the chance of what you say being understood by people who are able to receive that force. But if one speaks without thinking, usually it is impossible to understand what he says. It makes a kind of noise, that is all. For example, when you have the habit of speaking with someone, exchanging ideas with him, when between the two of you there is a certain mental adjustment, that is, when you have taken the precaution of saying, 'When I use this word I mean this', and so on; when you are used to an interchange, when you have established a kind of contact between brain and brain—even if it be only that— you understand each other quite easily. But with people who come altogether from elsewhere, with whom you have never spoken, you need a little time to adjust and adapt yourself to understand what they mean by the words they use. . . . What is it that makes you understand? It is just the kind of mental sense that is behind the words. When the thought is strongly thought out, there is a powerful vibration and it is that which is sensed; the word is only an intermediary means. . . . When there is a developed consciousness behind, when one has the power to concentrate it, one can do anything at all- this consciousness will act."[1]

When Mother settled here in India she did everything for, spoke for and aspired for India. All her words though relate to many countries are specially meant for India and her people. She intensely loved India. She taught the children of all age groups. She discussed with the leaders, teachers and sadhaks, disciples and others. She gave talks on occasions, wrote innumerable letters and messages. Meeting the visitors and sending blessings to the people on various occasions comprised her routine work, besides her other duties.

Sometimes such chores used to tax her health, particularly in later years, when her body was failing. People not only prayed for but even demanded her presence. Sometimes under compelling circumstances she complied with their demands. She seldom refused.

On most of the occasions she gladly met, blessed and gave them messages, when required. While many such letters, messages and talks were personal in nature and temporal in effect, many were universal in their appeal. They were national or international in their significance, as they came out of a divine consciousness. A few of her invaluable words are given below.

New Year messages had great significances for many who used to wait until she spoke out her New Year message, to begin the year. Some of them are given below:

1948

> Forward, for ever forward!
> At the end of the tunnel is the light
> At the end of the fight the victory!

1955

> No human will can finally prevail against the Divine's Will. Let us put ourselves deliberately and exclusively on the side of the Divine, and the Victory is ultimately certain.

1956

> The greatest victories are the least noisy.
> The manifestation of a new world is not proclaimed by beat of drum.

1960

> To know is good,
> to live is better,
> to be, that is perfect.

1970

> The world is preparing for a big change. Will you help?

Birthday messages were mostly personal and some were common like, "Let your life be useful." One such message has a unique appeal which we may keep in our heart to be repeated in each birthday:

> "A grain of practice is worth a mountain of theories."
>
> "Lord, on this anniversary day of my birth, grant that the power to know changes in me into a power to transform myself integrally."

She used to welcome Christmas as the festival of Lights. Her message for 1969 was:

> Hail the new light
> That it may grow in all hearts.
> Blessings.

Mother had spoken about some important countries, some important leaders, both national and international. It is known that many people for various reasons do not speak clearly about Tibet. Let us see what Mother said. On 18 January 1973 she received Dalai Lama, the spiritual leader of Tibet, and spoke highly about him. Later, on 20 January 1973 when questioned she said, "I told him Tibet would become independent again. He asked me, 'When?' I said, "I don't know."

"Sri Aurobindo's idea was an independent Tibet within a sort of great federation with India. But when will it be? I don't know.

In a message on 26 January 1963 Mother wrote: "True spirituality is not to renounce life, but to make life perfect with a Divine Perfection."

This is what India must show to the world now.

Elsewhere she wrote, "Humanity is a sick child always wanting what is bad for him. Philanthropy is like a mother who, in order to satisfy her child's demands, would give him the very thing that will make him worse.

"It is a mistake to consider service to humanity as the highest expression of service to the Divine. To do so is to remain far too confined within the limits of an exclusive human consciousness."

Mother was the pioneer of a new educational system. She was a great teacher. During her talks on 5 August 1965 her advice to the teachers was, "A teacher must absolutely possess the qualities and the consciousness which he wants to see his students acquire." Her advice to the Government was, "I would like the Government to recognise yoga as a subject of education . . . . because it will be good for the country.

"Matter will be transformed, it will be a solid base. Life will be divinised. Let Indians take the lead in the movement."

About the national language of India she had given her well considered opinion quite a few times. What she said during a long question-answer session with the teachers of the Centre of Education in Pondicherry on 11 November 1967 was very significant and valuable. It is so even today. She said:

"The ideal would be, in a few years, to have a rejuvenated Sanskrit as the representative language of India, that is, a Sanskrit spoken in such a way that . . . . Sanskrit is behind all the languages of India and it should be that. This was Sri Aurobindo's idea, when we spoke about it. Because now English is the language of the whole country, but that is abnormal. It is very helpful for relations with the rest of the world . . . here as soon as one begins to want a national language, everyone starts quarrelling . . . . no one could object to Sanskrit. It is more ancient language than the others and it contains the sounds, the root-sounds of many words . . . .

"Every child born in India should know it, just as every child born in France has to know French. . . . He has to know the national language . . . . I hope that a day will come when it will be possible."

On 15 December 1970 Mother made the following remark to Kireet Joshi, the then Registrar of the Sri Aurobindo International Centre of Education:

"Sanskrit should be the real national language. It is only Sanskrit which will be ultimately acceptable to the people of India. Sanskrit is the only language which creates an equal handicap for all the parts of the country, so that nobody has a natural advantage over others in learning it. When I speak of Sanskrit, it would be simple Sanskrit, but not 'simplified'.

"When India goes back to her soul, Sanskrit will naturally become India's national language."

Sri Aurobindo said that Hinduism, the Vedic religion in its earliest form, was the *Sanatana Dharma,* the mother of all religions. So we may feel Sanskrit as a world language. It is never really dead. Not only is it the mother of all Indian languages (doubt has been expressed about its status with respect to south Indian language), but it is connected to many European languages and South-East Asian languages as well. Sri Aurobindo said that Sanskrit and Tamil (the oldest extant language) had the same origin. All the South Indian languages are replete with Sanskrit words. Bhasa Indonesia, Bhasa Malayasia, Khmer Rouge, Sinhalese are close to Sanskrit. Lakshrmi Kanta Maitra, during the language issue in the Constituent Assembly, vehemently advocated the acceptance of Sanskrit as the national and official language. He said that it has the oldest and the most respectable pedigree of all the languages in the world. Professor Naziruddin Ahmed, Professor Sahidullah and many others had great respect for this language. They described it as the greatest, most wonderful and perfect language of the world. We also refer to the note of dissent, in the question of national language, by the renowned linguist of India, Dr. Suniti Kumar Chatterjee. European scholars like W.C. Taylor, Max Muller, and Sir William Jones paid high tribute to Sanskrit. Jones thought Sanskrit to be more copious and refined than Latin and Greek. Lakshmi Kanta Maitra also mentioned that such orientalists as Keith, Hunter, Colebrook, Schopenhauer, Goethe, Dubois and Mc. Donnell had accorded Sanskrit the highest place."[2]

It has been regretted that though 1999 was declared as the year of Sanskrit, precious little has been done about it. When we consider that Mother accorded the status of Soul-Language of India to Sanskrit, we understand why she wanted it to be India's national language for a future India; a spiritual guru of the world. We feel Sanskrit will be the symbol of india's national integrity.

Mother loved India as her motherland. She lived to complete the work assigned to her by Sri Aurobindo, the work of supramental manifestation and transformation. The sincerity of her wish to become an Indian officially would be understood from the statement given by her on 15 August 1954 on the occasion of Pondicherry's merger with India:

"I want to mark this day by the expression of a long cherished wish, that of becoming an Indian citizen. From the first time I came to India in 1914—I felt that India is my true country, the country of my soul and spirit. I had decided to realise this wish as soon as India would be free . . . . I am French by birth and early education, I am Indian by choice and predilection."

The Government of India did not grant her the dual nationality as Mother wanted. India in her vision was always a unified whole, undivided country. She had herself drawn a map of India in the Ashram Playground in 1951. Her brass symbol was fixed in the middle of it. It remains a part of the wall. About it she said on 29 July 1964, "The map was made after the Partition. It is the map of true India despite all fleeting appearances, and it shall always remain the map of true India, whatever people may think." She held that it was the spiritual body of India which was indivisible. In answer to a question on 18 September 1965 Mother said:

"When the division between India and Pakistan took place, Sri Aurobindo wrote very strongly: 'this division MUST go somehow or other,' by whatever means, he said. And to me he said, If they can't agree on doing it, they will fight."

Mother had a great reverence for India; she had a great role to play in the future world-order, she believed. She greatly valued Sri Aurobindo's ideas about India and allowed her thoughts to be shaped accordingly. Rather, she worked to fulfil Sri Aurobindo's vision about the future of India. Whenever the chance arose she sent her words to the Indian leaders to work for the unification of Mother India. The work could not be accomplished, in spite of the opportunities that had knocked at our door due to human weakness, she said later. A few of her messages and talks about India are given below.

Invocation (A message given on the occasion of India's independence):

"O our Mother, O Soul of India, Mother who hast never forsaken thy children even in the days of darkest depression, even when they turned away from thy voice, served other masters and denied thee, now when they have arisen and the light is on thy face in this dawn of thy liberation, in this great hour we salute thee. Guide us so that the horizon of freedom opening before us may be also a horizon of true greatness and of thy true life in the community of the nations. Guide us so that we may be always on the side of great ideals and show to men thy true visage, as a leader in the ways of the spirit and a friend and helper of all peoples."

Message given to Dr. Rajendra Prasad, President of India, "India must rise to the height of her mission and proclaim the Truth to the world.

"The Old World is an old world, in the true sense of the word 'old. India is much older, but she is more alive." (July 14 1962).

On 12 November, 1963 Mother was asked by a renowned weekly of India, along with other questions, what would be her vision of India. Mother replied: "India's true destiny is to be the Guru of the world."

Her message to President V.V. Giri on 14 September 1969 was: "Let us all work for the greatness of India."

To the Indian Prime Minister on 6 October 1969 she said through her message, "Let India work for the future and take the lead. Thus she will recover her true place in the world." After quoting her words given on different occasions, we should not forget what she herself said about her words, to understand the purport of them:

"Do not take my words for a teaching, always they are a force in action, attuned to a definite purpose, and they lose their true power when separated from that purpose."

Notes and References

1. *The Mother. Collected Works*. Centenary Edition. Pondicherry; Sri Aurobindo Ashram. 1979. V-5. pp.74-75.
2. Subhash C. Kashyap. Back to Sanskrit. *The Hindu*, dated 11.10.2000.

Works Cited

1. *The Mother. Collected Works*. Centenary Edition. Pondicherry; Sri Aurobindo Ashram. 1978. Volumes 12, 13, 15.
2. *India The Mother (A selection from Mother's words)*. Mysore; Mira Aditi 1988.

16

Mother's Work

While in her body, Mother entrusted certain works to certain persons according to the suitability of one's inner conditions, according to the necessity of time and place, which she must have reconsidered had she been a witness to it till today. From a letter of Sri Aurobindo dated 28.9.1933 we find that this point was hinted at. As for Mother, one will not find in her this blind adherence to an arrangement once made. ". . . There is a plasticity needed in the movement of time and the habit of life cannot afford to be rigid in its movements, otherwise life would either be turned into a mere mechanism or break to pieces."[1]

While any work done with proper perfection and consciousness of a karmayogi, selflessly offered to the divine, may become Mother's work, it is puerile to think whatever we do, may be in an institution she founded, to be her work, though we know that we do them just as any other work in life, with turbid mental and vital conditions and the work is to just fulfil our own need.

Does every institution not drift to a different point in the ever flowing current of human lives from its source or origin? Old elements many times rot and the new ones are mostly not properly oriented for who would orient them? Can we assume the position that whatever is happening, whether we are a part of it as a doer or not, we have nothing to do about it, as if it is her fault if the situation does not change or its conditions worsens? Has not Sri Aurobindo said in his *The Mother,* "Reject the false notion that the divine Power will do and is bound to do everything for you at your demand . . . .?"

We can quote more potent lines from Sri Aurobindo from another correspondence dated 17.10.1936, "Apart from incomplete sincerity, there is the difficulty that the brain is clouded by egoism and desire and imagines it is doing the very thing when it is doing something else. That is why I spoke of the danger of the theory of all from the Mother. There are people who have taken it that all that comes from their ego or the vital comes from the Mother, is her inspiration or what she has given them. There are others who have taken it as an excuse for going on in the old rut independently, saying that when the Mother wants she will change things! There were even some who on this basis created a subjective Mother in themselves whose dictates, flattering to their ego and desire, are pitted against the contrary dictates of the Mother here, and come to think that this external Mother is after all new and the real thing is the inner one or that she was putting them through an ordeal by contradicting the inner dictates and seeing what they would do! The truth remains the truth, but this power of twisting by the mind and other parts of the nature has to be kept in sight also."[2]

We cannot be inert and passive and call everything that we do as Mother's works. We cannot advise others to dedicate all their energies toward doing the works in the institutions founded by her or anywhere, assuming that these only are the Mother's works. Though it was her empire when she was on earth, we cannot limit the jurisdiction of the Universal Shakti, the Divine Mother to institutions, neither as they existed when she was present, nor as they stand now after her departure. All legitimate works done throughout the universe are her works, if done properly. We can not go for a new superstition, create a new slogan toward achieving our ends.

Regarding the dispute, if the emanations of the Mother are herself, Sri Aurobindo replied very clearly, "The Emanation is not a deputy, but the Mother herself. She is not bound to her body, but can put herself out (emanate) in any way she likes . . . . Its presence with the Sadhak is not dependent on his consciousness of it. If everything were dependent on the surface consciousness of the Sadhak, there would be no possibility of the divine action anywhere; the human worm would remain the human worm and human ass the human ass, for ever and ever. For if the Divine could not be there behind the veil, how could either ever become conscious of anything but their wormhood and asshood even throughout the ages?"[3]

In the chapter titled 'Sadhana through work for the Mother' in his book *The Mother*, compiled as excerpts from his letters, Sri Aurobindo said lots on the subject to make home his points to the disciples from time to time. If available in full, they would shed more light on the subject. Such things were mentioned elaborately in his *The Synthesis of Yoga*. Works for the Mother done with the right concentration on her is as much a *sadhana* as meditation and inner experiences. It is the same as doing yoga with karma or karmayoga. Based on them his ideas are given below:

"To go entirely inside in order to have experiences and to neglect the work as it is done with the external consciousness is to be unbalanced, one-sided in the Sadhana, for his Yoga is integral; so also to throw oneself outward and live in the external being alone is to be unbalanced, one-sided in the Sadhana. One must have the same consciousness in inner experience and outward action and make both full with the consciousness of the Mother. To do both meditation and work and dedicate both to the Mother is the best thing."

As for the work one does, there is no higher or lower work; all work is the same provided it is offered to the Mother and done for her and in her power. All ideas of ego, all association of egoistic feelings with the work must disappear. One begins to feel the Mother's force doing the work; the psychic grows through a certain inner attitude behind the work and the *adhara* becomes open both to the psychic intuitions and influences from within and to the descent from above. Then the result of meditation can come through the work itself.

When you can have constantly the feeling of a calm being within concentrated in the sense of the Divine Presence while the surface mind does the work, or when you can begin to feel always that it is the Mother's force that is doing the work and you are only a channel or an instrument, then in place of memory there will have begun the automatic constant realization of Yoga, divine union in works.

All work done in that spirit and with that consciousness becomes Karmayoga and can be regarded as part of his Sadhana. Sri Aurobindo wrote in *The Mother*, "Your only object in action shall be to serve, to receive, to fulfil, to become a manifesting instrument of the divine Shakti in her works."

The Mother always gives us hope, calls us to remain young and vigilant so that we can effectively collaborate with her. This is how she calls us through a message given to the All India Radio on her ninetieth birthday:

"It is not the number of years you have lived that makes you old. You become old when you stop progressing. As soon as you think you feel you have done what you had to do, as soon as you think you know what you ought to know, as soon as you want to sit and enjoy the results of your effort, with the feeling you have worked enough in life, then at once you become old and begin to decline. When, on the contrary, you are convinced that what you know is nothing compared to all that remains to be known, when you feel that what you have done is just the starting point of what remains to be done, when you see the future like an attractive sun shining with innumerable possibilities yet to be achieved, then you are young. . . . In peace and silence is the greatest strength."[4]

She herself confirmed the truth about her two selves on 10 October 1958, "On the one hand, there is what Sri Aurobindo—who, as the Avatar, represented the supreme Consciousness and Will on earth—declared me to be, that is, the supreme universal Mother; and on the other hand, there is what I am realizing in my body through the integral sadhana."[5]

Referring to the small book, *The Mother* (not the Volume 25 mentioned earlier which contains the book referred here), by Sri Aurobindo which is said to contain the quintessence of his philosophy and yoga, Sashi Bhusan Dasgupta in his article, 'Sri Aurobinder Sakti Sadhana'(Sanibarer Chithi, Aswin 1366 Bengali era) described his yoga path as a Tantrik sadhana. According to Sri Aurobindo, Dasgupta wrote, "The Mother, the eternal Shakti, in her earthly or lower self is ever preset on earth scene with an aspiration, an inclination to reach her higher nature. The earth nature has this emotion to reach the height as the Mother is involved here as an essential emotion, a light in darkness. For her everything is pushed toward the height. This is the hope of our evolution, of the transformation of the earth-nature, without which there would not remain any chance of change and progress.

"There is one divine Force which acts in the universe and in the individual and is also beyond the individual and the universe. The Mother stands for all these, but she is working here in the body to bring down something not yet expressed in this material world so as to transform life here—it is so that you should regard her as the Divine Shakti working here for that purpose. She is that in the body, but in her whole consciousness she is also identified with all the other aspects of the Divine."[6]

Mother in her two selves helps us to achieve the goal of reaching the divine. On our part we have to surrender entirely to her will so that she can push and pull us effectively, she can do the *sadhana*, living within us. This is our essential and real work, real service to the Mother.

Nolini Kanti a Gupta, a yogi and one of the oldest *sadhak* of the Ashram, a direct disciple of Sri Aurobindo and the Mother, was very close to her. He said on 21 November 1973, after the departure of the Mother:

"Mother once told me, 'If ever I leave my body my Consciousness will remain with you.'

"Mother is present among us and Her work continues. Let us once more dedicate ourselves for Her work of transformation with utmost sincerity and faithfulness."[7]

Knowing what she was according to her own realisation and according to Sri Aurobindo, knowing what her actual work was on earth; by the side of Sri Aurobindo and after his departure what remained to be done by her as a clear understanding between them, it should be clear what can be termed as Mother's Work to be done by her followers; those are surely not all day-to-day paraphernalia done to fulfil self-interest or done as a routine for the running of some organisation unless even those mundane works become really Works of the Mother in real terms so that they do not become undesirable or otiose.

Notes and References

1. Sri Aurobindo. *The Mother*. Pondicherry; SABCL, Sri Aurobindo Ashram. 1972. V-25. p.276.
2. *The Mother*. pp. 278-79.
3. *The Mother*. p.110.
4. *India The Mother*. Paris and Mysore; Institut de Recherches Evolutives and Mira Aditi. 1998. p. 173.
5. Satprem. *Mother's Agenda*. Paris; Institut de Recherches Evolutive. 1978. p. 209.
6. *The Mother*. pp. 49-50.
7. As reproduced in *The Mother: Past Present and Future*. K. D. Sethna. Jaipur; Kamal Printers. 1977. p. 156.

17

Mother Said

"It was an occasion of a host of silly events that occur constantly and make people repeat, 'Mother said, Mother felt, Mother did, Mother. ' I wondered, 'Can't I make them understand?' Well, I have seen that It's impossible, so I don't bother about it anymore. I simply said to those who have goodwill, 'Don't listen to what people tell you; when they come and tell you, Mother said, Mother wanted. Don't believe a word of it, that's all; let them say what they like, it doesn't matter. Mother said during one of her talks on 22 July 1964.[1] It seems that she was disgusted.

It is true that she said different things to different people, often contradictory, as per their differing inner needs. Many were her advices to individuals as per the then temporal needs, specific to their nature or situation. Some of her words were of universal nature carrying value for all, said on special occasions. Usually those are understood but they are on many instances misused. She explained it but gave up the idea of making people understand. It is fact that we often hear, "Mother said, Mother did, Mother wanted, but rarely do we hear," "Sri Aurobindo said or Sri Aurobindo wanted." There is difficulty in it and usually it is not as common as the Mother's day-to-day advices to her disciples or others as she would look after all arrangements, everyday needs.

Knowing Mother and her works are the first steps toward a movement to know her thoughts and ideas. Innumerable were the subjects she had spoken about. Concentrātion on a few controversial and important topics, about which she had repeated her statements, opinions and acted continuously to establish her ideas, may perhaps help us to clear the cloud. In this connection we have to remember that human actions stem from reactions whereas divine action is spontaneous; it speaks to each thing or being according to its dharma, by which Mother meant both law and truth. She confirmed that her actions were the result of neither mental nor vital nor emotional or physical reactions.

Religion and Spirituality

Mother was against any hollow ritualistic practices. She was ardently in favour of spirituality. On 23 May 1956, about her sojourn to India for the first time in a Japanese boat she gave a detailed report of how on a Sunday everyone crowded down into the lounge and the Presbyterian made a speech. Everybody listened very religiously and when it was over, they all came up again with the satisfied air of someone who has done his duty. And, of course, five minutes later they were in the bar drinking and playing cards, and their religious ceremony was forgotten; there was nothing more to be said about it.

When repeatedly insisted to speak her mind why she did not take part in it, she said to the clergyman, "I don't feel that you are sincere, neither you nor your flock. You all went there to fulfil a social duty and a social custom, but not at all because you really wanted to enter into communion with God."

Puzzled, the questioner uttered, "Enter into communion with God! But we can't do that!"[2]

Someone asked her permission to visit a church on 25 December 1969 to see the midnight ceremony. Mother replied that while Sri Aurobindo spent his whole life to free men from the bondage of religions, does he want to contradict his work for the sake of a childish curiosity? But we must remember from such examples that such perfunctory religiosity is found with most human beings belonging to any religious denomination. Most of them are not awake to their devotional or routine rituals done because in the absence of it they would feel vacant, feel afraid inwardly or as in most cases they would feel isolated from their group of general practitioners.

Let us see what Sri Aurobindo said about freedom from the bondage of religion, about the spirituality: "Spirituality is not a high intellectuality, not idealism, not an ethical turn of mind or moral purity and austerity, not religiosity or an ardent and exalted emotional fervour, not even a compound of all these excellent things. Spirituality is in its essence an awakening to the inner reality of our being, to a spirit, self, soul which is other than our mind, life and body, an inner aspiration to know, to feel, to be that, to enter into contact with the greater Reality—beyond and pervading the universe which inhabits also our own being, to be in communion with It and union with It, and a turning, a conversion, a transformation of our whole being as a new self of the aspiration, the conpact, the unions a growth or waking into a new becoming or new being, a new self, a new nature."[3]

A note from Mother dated 19 March 1973 was: Here we have no religion.

"We replace religion with spiritual life, which is truer and both deeper and higher, that is to say, closer to the Divine. For the Divine is in all things, but we are not conscious of it.

"This is the immense progress that men must make."[4]

Her oft repeated statement was again said on 5 April 1967, "What is most important, is to get rid of that division. And they all have it in their minds—each and everyone of them! The division between living a spiritual life or living the ordinary life, having a spiritual consciousness or having an ordinary consciousness—there is only One consciousness!

"It's still the old idea. Still the old idea of the sage, the yogi, the sannyasin, the . . . who represents spiritual life, while all others represent ordinary life- but it's not true! It's not true, not true at all,"[5] she stressed in elaborating it.

What she wanted to say is that it is not the denial of life by the sannyasin or the rigidity of rituals that should be our goal for our goal is much vaster; spiritual. As a conclusion she quoted Sri Aurobindo, from his *Essays on the Gita*, "We do not belong to the past dawns, but to the noons of the future."[6]

But we see that she spoke of the two consciousnesses too and differentiated between them at certain other times. Whatever ceremonies and festivals she participated, in whatever position, were gestures of her goodwill and benediction towards her disciples and devotees not for the festival or the occasion.

"The true spiritual life begins when one is in communion with the Divine in the psychic, when one is conscious of the divine Presence in the psychic and in constant communion with the psychic. Then the spiritual life begins, not before. . . .

"Before that, one may be an aspirant to the spiritual life, but one doesn't have a spiritual life, she said."[7]

"All that opens to us the road to the supreme realities, pulls us out from the mud of the Ignorance in which we are stuck, opens the door to us, shows us the path, leads us to where we have to go—this is what man has called 'Spirit'.

"In fact, the vast majority of men are like prisoners with all the doors and windows closed, so they suffocate, which is quite natural."[8]

"There are people who live constantly in a higher consciousness, while others have to make an effort to enter there."[9]

With an understanding of what is spiritual consciousness and what is not or what is ordinary consciousness we shall move to the most important action to attend spiritual consciousness.

Meditation

Some have the idea that Mother was against doing meditation, almost a compulsory discipline in every yogic, spiritual system. How could Mother, who used to spontaneously meditate for hours in the jungle of Fontainbleu in Paris during her teens, how could she, who used to meditate in the early morning for decades and note her experiences in her notebooks, later published as *Prayers and Meditations*, how could she who often entered into trance, who led and gave meditations to her disciples for years, who showed the greatest example of surrender during her silent meditation with Sri Aurobindo on 29 March when she first met him in 1914, show disregard for it? Let us see.

On 17 February 1951 she explained during the question hour that during the meditation session in the Ashram she used to try to kindle the flame of aspiration, to help it to rise up in her disciples and during Playground meditations she invited those who wanted the perfection of their physical body for the yoga. About the Ashram meditation she said, "I tried to unify the consciousness of all who were present and to lift it in an aspiration towards higher regions; it was a movement of ascent, of aspiration- whereas what we do here, in concentration, is a movement of descent. . . . .

"Who really want the perfection of their physical body can come, not those who want to escape from life, escape from themselves, escape from their body to enter into the heights."[10]

"With a little practice one reaches a state which may be obtained at will in a few seconds, that is, one doesn't waste any meditation time," she said on 5 June 1957. About the result she said, "It may be an illumination, an understanding truer or closer to the truth, or a power of transformation which helps you to achieve a psychological progress or a widening of the consciousness or a greater control over your movements, over the activities of the being."[11]

"Is not sitting down to meditation an indispensable discipline and does it not give a more intense and concentrated union with the Divine?" someone asked. Mother did not deny it. "That may be," she said. "But a discipline in itself is not what we are seeking. What we are seeking is to be concentrated on the Divine in all that we do, at all times, in all our acts and in every movement."

During her Question and Answer session in 1929 she said, "The number of hours spent in meditation is no proof of spiritual progress. It is a proof if your progress when you no longer have to make an effort to meditate . . . .

"There are some who have been asked to meditate; but also there are others who have not been asked to do any meditation at all . . . . To work, to act with devotion and an inner consecration is also a spiritual discipline. The final aim is to be in constant union with the divine, not only in meditation but in all circumstances and in all the active life."[12]

She stopped taking meditation for sometime for an atmosphere of formidable mass of stupid prejudices which created an irreconcilable antagonism between material and spiritual life, as she explained. This she considered to be foolishness which is to be uprooted to pave the way toward Supramental manifestation.

"What I most fear are those who believe themselves very exceptional because they sit down and meditate. they become so vain and so full of self-satisfaction that they close up in this way all avenues of progress. There is one thing that has always been said, but always misunderstood, it is the necessity of humility."[13]

She said, "Whatever work it is, if you do it and while doing it are careful not to forget the Divine, to offer to Him what you do and try so to give yourself to Him that He may change all your actions . . . then in that way you will make progress."[14]

"The Ashram is meant for yoga, not for musical entertainment or other social activities.

"Those that live in the Ashram are requested to live quietly and noiselessly and if they are not capable themselves of meditation they must, at least, leave the others to meditate," she said on 25 April 1958. [15]

She hastened to add that she liked music very much as she was a practising musician but said that it should be limited to a good atmosphere.

Sri Aurobindo insisted on meditation as a process of doing yoga. Mother never denied it. She herself was a great practitioner of it, but she disliked any pretence and demanded absolute sincerity. She felt that one would meditate when the real time arrived for him, almost under compulsion. She wanted sadhaks to always meditate and offer, in all circumstances, amidst all actions, which are much more difficult that usual meditation, she admitted.

In reply to some questions about sports and Mother's attention toward it, about the playground meditation, Sri Aurobindo made it clear that playground meditation was an ordinary concentration for physical exercise while meditation for spiritual development was guided by the Mother in the Ashram. He said that sports was given its due place but that could not take the place of *sadhana* in the Ashram. All these references are to confirm that Mother was never against meditation in favour of any work done for any purpose.

We may here verify Mother's views and actions on certain important social institutions and ceremonies, on human activities in collective and individual life to clear our faith on her which are contrary to what some say as Mother said.

Marriage is important in every society. It is the second important stage of life, Garhasthya ashrama, according to Hindu social system. Mother usually blessed the newly married couple or those going to be married. But her opinions are given below which throw sufficient light on the subject.

In a letter on 28 July 1937 she wrote, that she never advised anyone to marry; it is a terrible bondage. But she did not restrict anyone to marry. She gave them freedom saying that you are free and that it is for you to make the decision; that's all.

In a letter on 13 October 1940 she said, "Marriage is not a direct way to prepare oneself for sadhana. It can be an indirect one if the outward nature needs troubles and disappointments to get rid of worldly attachments."[16]

During her talks on 19 Octcber 1963 she mentioned, "I had the experience of a young couple who came to see me. "It has become a custom nowadays that young people who are going to marry and whose families I know, or who live here, come to receive my blessings before marrying! That's the new fashion" to receive my blessings. Then they went. And they left behind in the room a vital formation, very bubbly, absolutely ignorant, very bubbly with *a joie de vivre, a joie de vivre* so blissfully ignorant of all possible difficulties, all possible miseries, and not only for oneself but for everyone! (Note that these young people belong to the 'top' of society.) I wondered if it isn't even more widespread in Western countries than here—I think it is."[17]

During the same year Bharatidi, a French lady of 73, wrote to Mother, if she would have to marry to get an interview. Mother's reply was both humorous and penetrating:

"O Bharaitidi, our dear friend!

"Don't marry, it will be such a big loss for all—for you would have to leave the Ashram, at least during the honeymoon. My programme is generally five minutes of meditation, sometimes less—and how I ask you to climb two storeys for that. And your voice resounds at times to my inner hearing—and I always reply in the silence."

Generally it may be said that she advised someone or the other depending on their condition of life to marry or not to marry but it cannot be said that she viewed it as an ideal position for leading a life that she professed.

Rules and Regulations

Mother did not prescribe too many rules for her governance, for they give scopes for revolt. She expected that with the growth of spirituality in her disciples lower-nature and propensities to immoral things would fall off from their nature. However, for those who intended to practice integral yoga, she prohibited three things—sexual relation, drinking alcohol and smoking. She also prohibited politics.

Politics

Mother was always for organizing the country beyond politics. A party is like a box, a limitation. Taking the clue from what Sri Aurobindo said, she thought that "we represent no party! We represent India."

During talks she said, "I am not saying officially; because I have said and always repeat that politics is in complete Falsehood, based on Falsehood, and I am not dealing with it, meaning that I am not in politics, I don't want to be—but that doesn't stop me from seeing clearly!"[18]

If there is a man who feels like going in for politics, that is different; but I think the others will be strong without being inside, "she said on 25 May 1970."[19]

But she loved India, loved men. She would not leave any area of life unexplored, specially such an important area of country's progress, but not through politics. She was very clear on the point and advised, "It is to organise the country beyond politics. And it is the only way. . . .

"There is no hope in going backwards; it would make things last endlessly. We must go forward, absolutely, and go beyond, beyond party. And nobody can explain that better than Sri Aurobindo, because he was so much, so much beyond party; he saw the advantages and disadvantages of all parties and he stated them exactly."[20]

This journey of finding what Mother said and what she meant is very lengthy and repetitious, labyrinthine. I have tried to bring home some common areas where 'Mother Said is quite popular. A nice example will make the point acute.' "Do not trouble yourselves with what others do, I cannot repeat it to you too often. Do not judge, do not criticise, do not compare. That is not your lookout."(1957)[21]

If this were Mother's dictum for all it would be a paradise for the looters and whimsical actors, a playground for all wrong doers but fortunately the publisher of the volume 14, titled 'Words of the Mother' (*The Mother. Collected Works*. Centenary Edition. 1978.) wrote in his Note, "The reader should note that most of these statements were written for individuals under particular circumstances and were not, at the time of writing, intended for general circulation.

Still this write up is often put up for general consumption.

After many years of her departure Mother has become a myth and superstition; Mother's words, her smile, her Prasad are much in demand for multiple uses around her last abode and perhaps beyond. This is an effort to bring out what Mother actually said, what she intended her children to do, to become, to the extent possible, for deviations are part of life. She was Mother of love. She never refused anybody. She always smiled. Even when she was utterly busy, she received people, corresponded with a large number of them. A large number of people regularly met her in spite of her failing health, simply for the satisfaction of receiving her blessings, for a work or ritual, perhaps very personal and not so important generally. She could not refuse when people around her pushed them. Many received her Divine smile, flowers and other things during their sole visit to the Ashram. Many, who happened to be there, near her, received her smile, touch, blessings for days, months and years together, as the chance occurred during the days of her ministry.

Mother accommodated her children in many ways, giving relaxation to norms, showing special kindness to some out of benevolence. But perhaps she, only she, who knew the inner sides of everything and everyone, could do it. Let all those who received such bounty keep them as treasures in the special Chambers of their hearts. But that might neither be due to any speciality of the recipients' character nor their legitimate due but because they remained or occupied a physical nearness to her at that particular point of time. Wonderful was her world, from wonder she travelled to wonder.

Notes and References

1. Satprem. *Mother's Agenda*. Paris; Institut de Recherches Evolutive. 1988. V-5. p.133.
2. *The Mother. Collected Works*. Centenary Edition. Pondicherry; Sri Aurobindo Ashram. V-8. pp.149-150.
3. Sri Aurobindo. *The Life Divine*. Pondicherry; SABCL, Sri Aurobindo Ashram.Vol-19. p. 857.
4. *Mother's Agenda*. op. cit. V-13. p. 379.
5. *Mother's Agenda*. V-8. pp. 100 and 98.
6. *Mother's Agenda*. V-8. p. 103.
7. *The Mother*. V-8. p. 136.
8. *The Mother*. V-9. pp. 430-431.
9. *The Mother*. V-4. p. 230.
10. *The Mother*. V-4. pp. 122-123.
11. *The Mother*. V-9. p.115.
12. *The Mother*. V-3. p. 20.
13. *The Mother*. V-5. p. 45.
14. *The Mother*. V-5. p. 44.
15. *The Mother*. V-13. p. 120.
16. *The Mother*. V-14.p. 313.
17. *Mother's Agenda*. op. cit. V-4. pp. 358-59.
18. *India The Mother*. Paris and Mysore; Institut de Recherches Evolutives and Mira Aditi. 1998. p.146.
19. *The Mother*. V-15. p.467.
20. *The Mother*. V-15. pp.426-427.
21. *The Mother*. V-14. p.293.

18

Towards a Glorious Body

atmanam rathinam viddhi sariram ratham eva cha
buddhim tu sarathim viddhi manah pragraham eva cha

Know the body for a chariot and the soul for the master of the chariot:
Know reason for the charioteer and the mind for the reins only.

(*Katha Upanishad.* First cycle. Chapter No. 3.
Translation by Sri Aurobindo)

The divine Mother knew her soul. She conquered her mind, *vital* and reason.

Sri Aurobindo, the prophet of *Life Divine,* had achieved spiritual realisation long ago, on 24 November 1926. But he continued his *sadhana* for the descent of the Supramental force and consciousness upon earth. He left his body on 5 December 1950 in order to hasten the advent of the Supramental consciousness. The ancient Rishis might have had knowledge about the Supermind but none had envisaged its descent, none had an inkling about the transformation of life on earth, he said. After his departure it was Mother who carried on the work. Her work is a unique record in the spiritual history of the mankind.

While talking to Dr. Prabhat Sanyal on the morning of 6 December 1950, Mother said, "People do not know what a tremendous sacrifice He has made for the world. About a year ago, while I was discussing things I remarked that I felt like leaving this body of mine. He spoke out in a very firm tone,

'No, this can never be. If necessary for this transformation I might go, you will have to fulfil our yoga of supramental descent and transformation!'"[1]

In order to understand why he left his body and why Mother was asked to continue the *sadhana*, we have to understand the basic concept of Suprarnental consciousness (the word was coined by Sri Aurobindo) and why it was necessary to bring it down upon earth.

In his article '*The Divine Body*', Sri Aurobindo wrote that light, bliss, beauty and perfection of the right action of the whole being are the native power of the Supramental truth consciousness which will transform mind, life and body for a manifestation of a truth conscious spirit upon earth. Before him, he noted, no spiritual system regarded the body as capable of transformation, capable of spiritualisation. Many gurus regarded life and earth as maya or illusion. But his aim was total transformation up to the lowest matter in order to establish God in life. "If a total transformation of the being is our aim, a transformation of the body must be an indispensible part of it; without that no full divine life on earth is possible," he said.[2]

Sri Aurobindo felt that Mother's body was more appropriate for transformation. "But the divine body must be a continuation of the already developed evolutionary form, a continuity from the human to the divine. It will develop many subtleties and plasticities, a new process of acquiring knowledge, a new aesthesis, new potencies of manipulation of itself and objects. The transformation of the physical being might follow this incessant line of progression and the divine body reflect or reproduce here in a divine life on earth something of this highest greatness and glory of the self-manifesting Spirit."[3]

In the process of his Integral Yoga, Sri Aurobindo divided and subdivided the parts and planes of the human being. He said that there is a physical mind below the vital but it is linked with the mind proper which can act in its own sphere by a direct touch with the higher mental Intelligence. Besides this, there is an obscure mind of the body—of the cells, molecules, corpuscles.

Citing the example of Hackel, the German materialist, who thought that each atom has its will, and referring to the scientific discovery about the variation of activity in each electron, Sri Aurobindo said that there is a secret reality acting behind each thing like the atom, electron, cell and molecule. In fact, two American scientists, Dr. Alfred G. Gilman and Dr. Martin Rodbell won the Nobel Prize for their discovery of how the cells talk to each other.

Thus, the body-mind is a tangible truth but because it clings to the past movements and its rejection of the new and other obscurities, it stands as a stumbling block before the Supermind in its action towards the transformation of the body. But he asserted that its effective conversion by any means would make it the most precious instrument for the stabilisation of the Supramental light and force in material nature.

When Sri Aurobindo departed his body it was surcharged with a part of the Supramental force and consciousness, called 'The Mind of Light', which entered Mother's body. The function of this light was to purify the obscure body-mind. She carried on the work as she was assigned, till her last mortal day. Mother confirmed that the Supramental had been established in Sri Aurobindo's body as early as 1938 but it had not transformed his body.[4]

Mother, who had an aura of light above her head from an early age and who was often visited by those in the other world in her sleep and dream, had always been from her teens, in search of a higher truth that would dawn on earth one day. On 25 September 1914 she wrote in her diary:

> The Lord has willed and Thou dost execute:
> A new light shall break upon the earth,
> A new world shall be born,
> And the things that were promised shall be fulfilled.

This was after she had met Sri Aurobindo and realized the position. On 29 February 1956 when she had been guiding a meditation in the evening, the Supramental descent took place on earth. It was something tremendous, she later said. It was as if the gates of heaven had opened and the flood of light came pouring in. She witnessed it for 20 minutes and then stopped the meditation.

On 29 March 1956, with reference to the descent, she made few changes in her former diary note. The revised note read:

> Lord, Thou hast willed and I execute:
> A new light breakes upon the earth,
> A new world is born.
> The things that were promised are fulfilled.

Apart from other occult experiences, Mother had many great experiences at the Supermental. After a month's illness—a severe heart attack- she woke up on 13 April 1962 to relate her experience of the night before to her disciple. It was a supreme love that was manifesting itself through big pulsations. It was stupendous, all-engulfing, eternal love. She had the certitude that the supramental manifestation was realised.

> The skies are full of songs of victory.
> The Truth alone exists, it alone shall be manifested.
> Forward!
> Glory to Thee, Lord supreme Triumpher.[5]

On 10 July 1957 she again felt that a new world had been born. It was not the old one which was in the process of transformation. She often remained in contact with Sri Aurobindo in the subtle physical plane. He had become more powerful after leaving the body, Mother said. The Supramental Avatar constantly helped her to achieve the truth, Mother said on a number of occasions.

The descent of the 'Superman Consciousness' on her occurred at the midnight of 1 January 1969. A concrete and new consciousness surrounded her for two or three hours. It was the consciousness, intermediary between man and the Supramental being. It gave her perfect assurance and confidence.

The Supramental consciousness·directly entered into her, for the first time on 6 October 1959, she said. About the occasion she said, "I had a unique experience. The Supramental light entered my body directly . . . . This was for the first time. It came in through the feet ... A gold and red color, marvellous, warm, intense. And it rose and rose ... so did the fever . . . . And all of a sudden, there was a second when I fainted. I found myself in another world . . . ."[6]

The main trait of Mother's character was pragmatism. She was not satisfied with theories. She tried her utmost to experience every occult truth in her life. After her final arrival in India on 24 April 1920 she moved to Sri Aurobindo's house on 24 November of the same year when the roof of her house collapsed under the pressure of the cyclonic weather. After his siddhi on 24 November 1926, Sri Aurobindo said to his disciples who had gathered there:

"I called you to tell you that from today I am withdrawing for my sadhana and the Mother will take charge of everyone; it is she to whom you should address yourselves. She who will represent me, she who will do all the work."[7] Thus, she did all the work from the establishment of the Ashram to looking after the nitty-gritty of its day-to-day affairs. After the first phase of her sickness in November 1958 Mother retired from outdoor activities. But she continued to look after everything and guide her disciples from her room. Ever since his departure, Mother felt the absence of Sri Aurobindo deeply and expressed it thus:

"You cannot imagine what a grace it is to have someone you can totally rely on, to let yourself be led with no need to look for anything. I had that, I was very conscious of that as long as Sri Aurobindo was here, and when he left his body, it was a terrible collapse . . . . You cannot imagine . . . . There is no path, the path must be made."[8]

In 1965 she said that the severest test she had been given was Sri Aurobindo's departure. Though she did not find the path immediately, when she finally did later, she fought with every drop of her blood to follow it, to establish the truth, to transform matter to bring divine life upon earth, it was a work mainly on her own body. About the body, she said, "that there are various kinds of freedom—vital, mental, spiritual—but a completely new freedom is the freedom of the body. . . . it's not a higher consciousness imposing itself on the body: it's the body itself awakening in its cells, it's a freedom in the cells."[9]

"One has the spiritual experience that material life is an illusion ... but now, it's the whole spiritual construction as we have lived it that has become a complete illusion!"[10]

She had been searching for a mantra immediately after her retirement in 1958 as she believed that the sound of it would create a vibration in the cells of the body which would become conscious with a tremendous concentration. Once she got the mantra in 1958—'Om Namo Bhagabateh'; it began to repeat itself. The cells were repeating the mantra continuously. All the cells of the body were seized with all intensity of aspiration. Her whole body swelled sometimes to the point of bursting. Though she realised that the body's texture is made of ignorance, requiring purification to receive the divine light, force and power, she had proof about the omnipresence of the supreme in the most unconscious matter.

She was undergoing various changes in her body, apart from in other parts of her being. She had a series of heart attacks in 1962 and 1970 and had other illnesses in her teeth, stomach and other parts of her body, which she usually cured with her yogic power. She would often remain in trance. Probably in the absence of such a spiritual personality as Sri Aurohindo, she often felt shaky and perhaps irritated, about her human surroundings. Scientists have discovered that the cell is the structural and functional—both organisational and developmental—unit of the body. On one side there are unicellular organisms like bacteria and fungi on earth, on the other, there is the most complex organism, the human body, which contains some 50 trillion cells. Cells are the chemical factories in the body. No living body can function without them. Life is a journey from cell to cell.

Nobel Laureate scientists Dr. Alfred G. Gilinan and Dr. Martin Rodbell discovered that cells talk to each other through G-Proteins. According to a recent report, an Israel scientist has expressed the hope that within two decades, cells in the human body may be programmed to act like tiny biological computers to detect the intruding hostile bacteria, diagnose the imminent disease and release the necessary quantity of antibiotic to fight it.

Scientists have observed immense possibilities of growth and development through cells in their own technical way. But Mother looked at the other aspects of the cells. She found that each cell is a unit of consciousness. She did not think that consciousness originated in the brain. She realised like Sri Aurobindo that everything in creation is conscious; dormant or wide awake. She wanted to put the spark of divine light into them so that they would become transformed to hold aloft a divine, immortal body, heralding a life divine upon earth. The transformation of the cells of her body gradually became her main occupation.

"One must die to death in order to be born to immortality . . . death no longer has any reality," she said on 4 July 1962.[11]

Again on 16 March 1963 she said, "Death is not the opposite of life. It's a sort of change in the cells functioning, or in their organisation."[12]

On the basis of her continued experiments she felt, "Death is the decentralisation of the consciousness contained in the body's cells . . . . The very first step toward immortality is therefore to replace the mechanical centralisation by a willed centralisation."[13] In an advanced stage of her *sadhana* of the body, on December 9, 1972 she realised that it was neither death nor life, it was something else that was divine. On October 14, 1953 she said that death was not inevitable, it was an accident. But this human habit is so old that it would take a great warrior to fight against it. It would be a battle against millions of adversaries. A few descriptions from the battlefield would be appropriate.

On January 9, 1962 she said that her illness was the result of a strange attack, not dependent on health. Whereas usually the cells remain concentrated around a centripetal force, it was the opposite in her case. The centrifugal force had caused them to scatter. When it became too much, she left her body. It seemed as if she had fainted, but she was actually fully conscious. After three days she felt that her problem was a maladjustment with the cells, which was not the case of ill health as ordinarily people or doctors suppose. She usually disliked doctors treating her, but she could not protect herself from their care as she had protected Sri Aurobindo. Disciples were usually worried about her health. The only reality of the physical world was pain, which she considered to be a falsehood but she could not cure herself with her yogic force as before. It seemed that someone else had taken charge of her. And she surrendered.

On August 9, 1963 she had a series of fantastic cellular experiences between 8.30 pm and 2.30 am. Her body became a forest, a house, a river, a mountain. All this was concrete experience. Her ways of looking at things, doing and feeling were changing. She looked at the vibration, force going through a person. Other physical features were otiose, false to her. She could not thread a needle at that time usually, but if it was so needed, it threaded itself. She could not hear people, but those she heard who were required at the point of time. So was the need to communicate, which was done with complete precision up to the point it was required. All this was innate knowledge without complications, hinting toward a Supramental world. Her body became others' bodies. She suffered their pains. Once haemorrhage disturbed her body. After it was over she received a letter that someone had been suffering from that ailment which was by that time cured. We remember Sri Ramakrishna suddenly suffered lashing on his back at a time when a bullock was whipped elsewhere.

On 20 July 1968 she said, "I don't know how many times a day, there will suddenly come the awareness of a disorder, a pain or suffering somewhere."[14]

She went very deep into the regions of the cells. It was a frightful state of anguish because it was nothing. She could not get out of nothingness and that was the foundation of all materialism, she said on 21 August 1963. Her body suffered when she plunged into the subconscient from time to time. But the cells were ready to struggle for centuries, she understood on 16 October 1962. She often fainted between the years 1962 and 1967 as she had been struggling to come out of the web of physical consciousness, the body-mind and all sorts of minds.

She wanted to break the habit of the millennia. Sometimes she was not sure what was happening inside her. Her body was sometimes moved at fantastic speed and remained static at the same time. It was such intense speed that it seemed motionless. The experience was both yogic and atomic.

On 31 May 1969 she said, "All the methods . . . . Nirvana included—all the methods to get out of it are worthless. I don't know. But salvation *is physical*—not at all mental, but physical. I mean it's not in escape: it's here . . . . All the rest, including death, really becomes a falsehood, that is to say, something that does not exist."[15]

Even in 1966 she felt that parts of her body had been changing. Sometimes her body was in a state of immortality, but it was not constant. It depended on other things and the moment it depended, the Supreme's assurance was gone. After a continued struggle to free her body from the web of different levels of mind, from 1958 to 1968, the mind that tried to pull her down, she realised that the real work was done by Sri Aurobindo:

"Now I understand. And I see, I see now how his departure and his work—so immense, you know, and constant, in that subtle physical—how much that has helped. How he helped prepare things, change the structure of the physical. Truly, it's not as it was—it is no longer as it was."[16]

She was uncertain as to what was exactly going to happen. On April 1 970 she said, "A very very strange sensation . . . . A mystery of the unknown. And that's becoming constant ... it realises that that vibration is not one of dissolution, but something—What? The unknown, completely unknown- new, unknown."[17]

Another day she felt that her body was no longer a part of the old being, but it knew that it still was not in the new way. It was no longer mortal or immortal. She travelled from a most dreadful discomfort to a marvel. She admitted that she was plunged in a world that she did now know. It was strange. She was stupefied. But she was not going to stop. She was constantly struggling to hew a new path for herself, for the body, for all bodies. Her agony, even emanating from others, could be felt from the courtyard below her window in the second floor.

"All those who were in the courtyard below must have heard how we had to fight with Her to make Her eat a little. This continued for quite a long time,"[18] wrote Pranab Kumar Bhattacharya, one of the main attendants of the Mother. About feeding the Mother, the talk between Dr P. Sanyal and Mother, just after Sri Aurobindo's departure, comes to our mind:

"I was talking with the Mother, in Her room. In my own foolish way I voiced my apprehension for her health and the strain She put on her fragile frame. She smiled at me and asked, "Do you think I get all this energy from my frugal meals? Of course not, one can draw infinite energy from the universe when needeed!"[19]

In February 1970 Mother remarked, "There is a curious thing: I don't sleep and I am not awake. It's neither one nor the other. I am in a sort of new state . . . . What is it? I don't know . . . . And I am not out of my body. Or else the body is replaced by another one? I don't know."[20]

On another occasion she said that her the then body which belonged to the old creation was growing smaller, while her consciousness was growing vast, tall and powerful. She knew that the last thing to be changed, which the people were looking at, was the body, to believe that something was really happening. During the most part of 1971 and 1972, or even earlier, she had been progressively feeling the pressure of what Sri Aurobindo called the Supramental. It was unbearable at times and suddenly she caught a glimpse of a marvellous horizon. But she always concentrated on the cells of her body—for a change of consciousness in them.

"This mind of the cells which is mine now ... is being converted very fast and in a very interesting way ... all the memory that came from the mental knowledge went way a long long time ago ... But now a kind of memory is being built from below."[21]

There is a definite shift, a transfer of power, she felt. The nature was giving way to another authority. And Mother was constantly surrendering, her mantra being repeated automatically in the cells of the body; they were being transformed day by day.

Mother disliked death. To accept it was a defeat, she felt. She was going through a tremendous battle against death. She was building up a separate body in the subtle world while her own body was undergoing changes. It is certainly a story of the occult world but it could not be otherwise. Even to a stark materialist what she did throughout her life was very tangible, although they did not always conform to the usual cause and effect. What she experienced was hers only; none could share them after Sri Aurobindo's departure.

Each one who was very close to her for various needs and reasons, thought that he or she was very special to her. She behaved intimately with each one of them, spoke and wrote to them. She laughed with everyone who met her. But unfortunately, knowingly or unknowingly, many times they acted against her progress, against the serious works that continuously engaged herself in. Many have compared her to the protagonist of Sri Aurobindo's epic poem, *Savitri.* She herself said that what Sri Aurobindo wrote were facts of her life in many respects. Savitri's fight with Yama was equal to Mother's battle against Death. In *Savitri* the poet wrote:

> A day may come when she must stand unhelped
> On a dangerous brink of the world's doom and hers,
> Alone with death and close to extinction's edge,
> Her single greatness in that last dire scene,
> She must cross alone a perilous bridge in Time
> And reach an apex of world-destiny
> Where all is won or all is lost for men.[22]

Let us now see how she was building her second body as a strategy. Once in the year 1970 Mother remarked that something was trying to develop in the body, "I mean a way of being of the cells that would be the beginning of a new body. When it comes it produces a strange sensation . . . . The body itself feels it is going to die ... only a state of very intense faith makes it possible to withstand. As if one thing was being changed into another . . . . Something entirely new."[23]

This she herself was actualising for a little earlier she had said, "All this work of transformation of the cells, of the consciousness in the cells, seems to have to be wasted since the body will disintegrate . . . . There is a way, which is to prepare within oneself, before death, a body with all the transformed, illumined conscious cells—to assemble and form them into a body with the maximum number of conscious cells- and once that is completed, the consciousness enters that body and the other one can dissolve- it doesn't matter anymore."[24]

She saw that body in 1970 itself. "Well I saw my body! What it will be like. It's quite good. A form that looked like our own body, but without sex, that is, neither man nor woman. It's not such a different body, but so refined . . . . I had a color . . . somewhat like Auroville's color (orange), like that, but vibrant . . . not luminous, but with a sort of luminosity. And I was wide awake. I wasn't asleep; it was not a dream."[25]

At another time she said, "Previously I used to go into an inner state of being (I know and have experienced them all; I had a conscious life), but all that is over, finished. It's finished. It's as if . . . the physical became double. Two worlds, one within the other. Two levels of physical reality."[26]

On 24 March 1972 she saw her transformed body, "For the first time, early in the morning, I saw myself, my body—I do not know whether it was the Supramental body or . . . a body in transition . . . altogether new . . . it was sexless . . . . It was very slim—it was pretty. Truly a harmonious form."[27]

Though in 1972 she said that she had seen her body for the first time, as above, earlier in 1970 also she had seen it and talked about the double bodies. That it had been her second vision was confirmed by the interviewer and recorder of her talks, Satprem, on 24 March 1972 in '*Mother or The Mutation of Death- 3*', as referred elsewhere. She did not know the details of transition but instead of this body becoming the other, the other will become this one, she said. She later confirmed that such a second body was formed in the subtle physical, which one cannot see with physical eyes.

Long ago, on 4 December 1957, she had considered the same question about her second body, "Can we hope that this body . . . will have the possibility of being progressively transformed into something that will be able to express a higher life, or will we have to abandon this form altogether to enter another form which, as yet, does not exist on earth?"[28]

What had been a question in 1957 became almost a certainty in 1972-73. In April 1973 Mother fell so sick that she could no more continue to meet people. From 20 May Satprem, the recorder of her talks, was no more allowed to interview or record her talks. It seemed that she lost control over her body. She felt disturbed on many occasions as her attendants tried to feed her as per doctor's advice. On many occasions she expressed that her body was out of the preview of doctors.

Pranab Kumar Bhattacharya, who along with a few others closely attended on and nursed Mother up to the end, gave a talk on 4 December 1973 after Mother's departure. A few observations of Pranab would help us to better understand the position as it was in 1973, the last year of Mother's life.

Sometimes she took food and sometimes refused it. At times she was strongly persuaded to take it. On 10 November she developed a kind of hiccup which occurred after lunch and dinner. But it had been observed 8 or 10 days before which lasted for a short while. Her heart started failing and she had many other ailments. She remained extremely weak. From 13 November she asked her attendants to lift her shoulders, then her legs and then the whole body. They obeyed her throughout the night up to 4 am in the morning of the 14th. On that day they were asked to help her walk besides lifting her body. They tried but she failed to walk. Her lips became blue and her body grew white and pale. She staggered, almost collapsed. Thereafter they did not try it again. But they lifted her up. She said, "Pranab, lift me up and make me walk. My legs are getting paralysed; if you help me to walk again, they will be all right. But they did not listen. "Lift me up," she often said. And they obeyed.

On the 17th she was found lifting her hands and making some strange sounds (During her talks in April of the same year she had felt like screaming. Something so new was approaching that her body was afraid!). Even after 6.30 in the evening she asked them to lift her up, more than once. And it was done. At about 7 pm she made same strange sounds and her head was moving in a certain way which evoked suspicion. Dr. Sanyal, who had signed Sri Aurobindo's death certificate, was again called in. Her heart was beating at long intervals. Respiration was still there, but all stopped slowly. Doctor's external heart massage had no effect. He examined and declared that Mother had left her body at 7.25 pm. Some knowledgeable people later contended that it was at 7.26 pm. It was said that a timepiece stopped moving at that time in the Ashram school founded by her. Earlier, a clock had stopped at the time of Sri Aurobindo's departure.

What Pranab Bhattacharya said about Mother's departure is very relevant. He held that the inevitable, uncontrolled physical laws were more responsible than anything else. On one side she had to fight the onset of decay and old age and on the other She was fighting against this dirt that we were constantly throwing upon Her. It is true that she had to fight against too many ailments apart from old age. She had an invincible will, a lofty mission and one of the strongest determination along with mental and vital strength. She never verbally gave any indication that she wanted to go. "She tried, she fought and she suffered and showed us how suffering could be taken, "Pranab said. She fought up to the last moment. Even half an hour before passing away she wanted her body to be lifted. She wanted to walk. She had known that her body was a part of the old creation so she created another body, though in another plane.

Mother was both human and divine. Her human self entirely surrendered to the Lord. She had been faithfully doing the work assigned to her by Sri Aurobindo. It was their joint work. Though he was sure of her purpose, confident about what she was doing, she was never dogmatic about her remaining on earth. For after all, it was something unheard of in the spiritual history of the earth. It will be pertinent to discuss about the hint that she had given about the possibility of her leaving the body or acting otherwise if circumstances arose. In the middle of a conversation once in 1967, Mother suddenly asked her disciple to take a note. She dictated: 'Because of the necessities of the transformation, this body may enter a state of trance that will appear cataleptic. Above all, no doctors! Do not hasten, either to announce my death and to give the Government the right to intervene. Keep me carefully sheltered from all injuries that may come from outside—infection, poisoning etc.—and have untiring patience; it may last days, perhaps week, perhaps even longer, and you will have to wait patiently for me to come naturally out of that state once the work of transformation is accomplished."[29] This was distributed to five people immediately around her.

During his talk Pranab said that Mother had told him once in 1948, "When Sri Aurobindo was still living, she told me, '1 am not willing to go, I will not go, and this time there will be no tragedy; but if it so happens that I leave my body, then put my body under the Service Tree' (a copper pod tree, so named by Mother). When Sri Aurobindo's body was being placed in the Samadhi, under the above Service Tree, Mother asked her disciple to make two chambers in the Samadhi vault. The one above Sri Aurobindo's body was kept vacant.

On 30 December 1972 Mother was asked by her disciple and interviewer, "Do you feel anything for this year? After a silence Mother replied, Things have taken an extreme form. So there is, as it were, an uplift of the atmosphere towards a splendour . . . inconceivable, and at the same time the feeling that at any moment one may . . . one may die—not 'die', but the body may be dissolved. And so the two at the same time form a consciousness (Mother shakes her head) . . . all the old things seem puerile, childish, unconscious- within there . . . it is tremendous and wonderful."[30]

All this statements and hints suggest that anything might happen, though she had never wished to leave her body in spite of extreme suffering. She had completely surrendered to the Lord for the final result of her works.

The circumstance at the time of her leaving the body was, as Pranab described, "It looked to me as if a candle was slowly extinguishing."[31] Her disciples were aware of Mother's wishes about her departure. The body was brought down at 2 am, after almost seven hours of her departure and it was placed in the Samadhi at 10.30 am on 20 November 1973, after more than two and half days of her departure.

Mother was apprehensive of her body's failure to carry her, the Divine Mother, up to the last, in her effort to transform the body. Her fear about the wastage of all works done in the realm of the cells, once the body failed, was allayed by herself through her construction of a new body. It seems unlikely that she entered into a trance on 17 November 1973 in the circumstances as described. But occult truth is beyond the comprehension of the non-adept. In any case, she knew the technique of coming out of the body, had the circumstances so demanded. It also seems unlikely that she would reappear in a mortal way within a predictable time.

Though a few differing ideas have been expressed by her disciples—writers and thinkers—the subject of her passing away remains a mystery. One thing seems true to all her ardent disciples and devotees that Mother is still present among them—helping and guiding—then, as always. And what happens gradually, the ardent faith has diluted to superstition while work is going on the way they desire throwing the burden of all results upon the Mother. The Mother of tremendous action, will, love and practical reasoning with spiritual sense has become a myth.

We shall conclude our subject by quoting Nolini Kanta Gupta's observation on her final departure. This message displayed on the Notice Board and then published here and there.

"The Mother's body belonged to the old creation. It was meant to be the pedestal of the New Body. It served its purpose well. The New Body will come . . . . For a new mutation, a new procedure was needed. 'Death' was the first stage in that process . . . .

"Mother has prepared for us her New Body in the inner world, in the subtle physical which is as living and tangible as her physical body even though not as concrete . . . . That body she has built up in her long arduous labours, built up in a complete form and left with us and with humanity.

"The New Body of hers, prepared behind the material curtain, she sought to infuse into the material form, even press into it or force into it this new element; but matter and man's physical nature were not very ready; Earth still considered it as an intrusion, as something foreign. The material casing broke in consequence- perhaps not broke down, rather broke through, but that must be another story. But it is there, living and glorious in its beauty and power and is still at work within us and around us in the world, incessantly, towards the final consummation of its material embodiment."[32]

Notes and References

1. Dr. Prabhar Sanyal. A Call from Pondicherry. Pondicherry; *Mother India*, December 1991.
2. Sri Aurobindo. *Collected Works*. Pondicherry; SABCL, Sri Aurobindo Ashram. 1972. V-16. p.24.
3. Ibid. p.40.
4. K.D. Sethna. *The Mother: Past Present and Future*. Jaypur; Kamal Gambhir, 1977. p. 153.
5. Ibid. p.147.
6. Satprem. *The Mind Of The Cells*. Mysore; Mira Aditi, 1999. p. 176.
7. As quoted in Satprem's Mother or the Divine materialism. New York; Institute for Evolutionary Research, 1976. p.321.
8. Satprem. *Mother or the New Speeies-2*. New York; Institute for Evolutionary Research. 1983. p. 152.
9. Satprem. *The Mind Of The Cells*. p. 145.
10. Satprem. *The Mind Of The Cells*. p. 167.
11. Satprem. *The Mind Of The Cells*. p. 189.
12. Satprem. *The Mind Of The Cells*. p. 190.
13. Satprem. *The Mind Of The Cells*. p. 149.
14. Satprem. *The Mind Of The Cells*. p.60.
15. Satprem. *The Mind Of The Cells*. p. 111.
16. Satprerm. *Mother or The Mutation of Death-3*. New York; Institute for Evolutionary Research, 1987. p. 44.
17. *The Mind Of The Cells*. op. cit. pp. 198-199.
18. Pranab's Talk of 4.12.1973. Mother India, Pondicherry. December 1973 (supplement).
19. Dr. Prabhat Sanyal. op. cit., Pondicherry. December 1991.
23. *The Mother Or The Mutation Of Death-3*. pp. 57-58.
24. *The Mother Or The Mutation Of Death-3*. pp.89-90.

25. *The Mother Or The Mutation Of Death-3*. p. 100.
26. *The Mother Or The Mutation Of Death-3*. p. 196.
27. *Collected Works Of The Mother*. Pondicherry; Sri Aurobindo Ashram Trust. 197 V- 1I. p. 301.
28. *The Mind Of The Cells*. p. 17.
29. *The Mind Of The Cells*. p. 212.
30. *Collected Works of The Mother*. op.cit. p.330.
31. Pranab's Talk of 4-12-1973. On The Mother. Supplement to Mother India. December 5, 1973. This refers to all the references to the talk as mentioned in the chapter.
32. *Collected Works of Nolini Kanta Gupta*. Pondicherry; SAICE, Sri Aurohindo Ashram. 1974. Volume-5 (Sweet Mother).